MY HAIR IS PINK
UNDER THIS VEIL

MY HAIR IS PINK UNDER THIS VEIL

RABINA KHAN

Biteback Publishing

First published in Great Britain in 2021 by
Biteback Publishing Ltd, London
Copyright © Rabina Khan 2021

ISBN 978-1-78590-646-6

10 9 8 7 6 5 4 3 2 1

A CIP catalogue record for this book is available from the British Library.

Set in Minion Pro and Trade Gothic

Printed and bound in Great Britain by
CPI Group (UK) Ltd, Croydon CR0 4YY

In memory of my father

CONTENTS

PROLOGUE

In 1977, one of the girls in my infant school in Kent asked me if I was a golliwog. I said I wasn't sure, because I didn't know what a golliwog was.

In 2015, when I stood as an independent candidate for mayor in Tower Hamlets, a smartly dressed middle-class man saw me wearing a headscarf and asked me what colour my hair was underneath it.

I gave him a big smile. 'Pink,' I replied.

Did I win his vote? I rather doubt it.

I was a child of five without a head covering in 1977 and a woman in a headscarf in 2015, with the confidence to respond to the man intent on being unpleasant to me. The transition from a feisty young girl, doing mostly as she was told, but still being outspoken, to an independent, confident Muslim woman in the public eye has been one of tears, laughter and immense challenges. This book draws on those experiences and, I hope, will encourage other women of faith to play pivotal roles in tackling stereotypes and inequality.

So, who is the British Muslim woman?

How does she define herself?

How does she see the future for our people and our country?

Post-9/11, communities described as British Bangladeshi or British Pakistani increasingly found themselves referred to as 'Muslim', even though, as with all religions, there are practising and non-practising British Bangladeshis and Pakistanis.

Orthodox Jews, traditionally dressed, are called 'observant Jews'. When Hindu ladies wear bright saris, they are described as colourful. Buddhist monks in saffron robes are thought of as serene and passive. But a woman in a veil is often treated with suspicion, because the headscarf is seen as a symbol of extremism or oppression.

Sara Khan, former head of the anti-extremist organisation Inspire – let me repeat that word, anti-extremist – has described being 'spat on in the street' when she wears a headscarf. People have approached indignantly and sworn in her face. One man in a Union Jack T-shirt called her 'Osama bin Laden's wife'. One of her friends had dog faeces dropped on her head. Another woman, who relayed her experience to Sara, was waiting for the bus when a man punched her in the face in a completely unprovoked attack, giving her a black eye.

These are just a few examples of attacks that occur

nationwide. In July 2018, the monitoring group Tell MAMA reported a record number of anti-Muslim attacks, with women disproportionately targeted, primarily by male teenage perpetrators.

Let me stress two further points. It is only a small minority of individuals who threaten and attack Muslims; and it is only a minority of Muslim leaders and teachers who have twisted Islam to suit their own questionable agendas, creating fear and division and, in turn, causing all Muslims to be judged negatively and treated unjustly. As a comparison, when a minority of Christians commit fundamentalist terror attacks, it does not create similar levels of mistrust and segregation. Many people will remember Anders Breivik, the Norwegian right-wing extremist who murdered seventy-seven innocent people in 2011 when he detonated a bomb in central Oslo and then opened fire at an island youth camp. He claimed the attacks were necessary in order to stop the 'Islamisation' of Norway. Similarly, in August 2019, another young Norwegian, Philip Manshaus, entered a mosque just outside Oslo and opened fire, apparently inspired by Breivik as well as the terrorists behind the attacks in Christchurch, New Zealand, and El Paso, Texas.

Since that world-changing day when al-Qaeda flew aeroplanes into the Twin Towers in New York, the topic of Islam, Muslims and extremism has been debated repeatedly. Female Muslims and their style of dress have emerged as a key focus of media attention and Muslim women have become an easy target, suffering abuse and violence.

After 9/11, when attacks on Muslim communities became more prevalent, many Muslim women who had previously been ambivalent about the veil started to wear traditional Muslim clothes, whether the hijab, the niqab or even the burqa. (There is sometimes confusion among non-Muslim people surrounding Islamic clothing for women and what it is called, as there are several different names to describe each garment. The burqa is the most concealing of Islamic veils and is a loose, one-piece outer garment that covers the entire face and body, leaving just a mesh screen to see through. The niqab, on the other hand, is a veil that covers the hair and face but leaves the eyes uncovered, although it can be worn with a separate eye veil. The hijab is a scarf that fully covers the head and neck but leaves the face clear. Meanwhile, the jilbab is a long, loose-fitting coat that covers the whole body except the face. The abaya is a floor-length, long-sleeved over-garment that covers the body, except the head, but can be teamed with a hijab.) They did so not to please the imam or their male relatives, but in defiance of those who spat at, swore at and criticised women in headscarves.

In 2012, Danny Boyle's hugely powerful and resonant Olympics opening ceremony portrayed Britain as a land that is tolerant, fair and accommodating of the many tribes, lifestyles and beliefs it houses – a rainbow paradise. However, a rainbow is also an illusion. Naturally, these occasions have to be positive and have become more elaborate over the years, with each country promoting the best side of their nation and, some might suggest, trying to outdo other countries. Britain's 2012 ceremony concealed the darker elements of our society – the racism, alienation and inequality.

In 2015, three schoolgirls from east London travelled to Turkey before crossing the border into Syria to join ISIS. They were born in England and came from loving families, yet they felt so disenchanted that they believed their lives would be more fulfilling under a brutal terror regime in a war-torn country. We can only assume that this disenchantment made them vulnerable to radicalisation, although many reasons have been presented in various studies conducted on this issue.

By contrast, in the same year, Nadiya Hussain was the popular winner of *The Great British Bake Off* and was asked to bake a cake for the Queen's ninetieth birthday the following year. Since then, she has appeared on numerous TV shows, become a columnist for *The Times* and forged a career as a successful author. In 2017, she was named by Debrett's as one of the 500 most influential people in the UK – but even she has been forced to endure the racial abuse that has been part of her life for years.

In 2018, Boris Johnson said he opposed banning veils in public but that it was 'absolutely ridiculous that people should choose to go around looking like letter boxes'. Mr Johnson's reckless comment shows that the hostility Muslim women face exists across society including, disturbingly, emanating from the nation's leader. We should therefore recognise the immense fortitude of Muslim women who have fought against harsh judgement, discrimination and abuse to carve out successful careers.

Two of Britain's top television journalists, Mishal Husain of the BBC and Fatima Manji of *Channel 4 News* are authoritative and self-confident women, skilled at getting to the root of the political issues their interviewees are promoting. They show that Muslim women can observe their religion while working in the public eye. Mishal Husain does not wear a head covering; Fatima Manji was the first woman to report on British television wearing a hijab. They may have made opposite decisions on how they want to present themselves to the world, but both are equally good examples of modern Muslim women.

Mishal Husain told Zoe Williams in an interview in *The Guardian* in August 2018, 'With a name like mine, my career would only have been possible in Britain.' That is a good definition of Britain.

The same can be said for Shabana Mahmood, Yasmin Qureshi and Rushanara Ali who made history in 2010 by becoming three of the first Muslim women to win seats in Parliament, all for Labour; Shabana for Birmingham Ladywood, Yasmin for Bolton South East and Rushanara Ali for Bethnal Green and Bow. They followed Baroness Sayeeda Warsi, who was raised to the peerage in 2007, serving as Conservative Party co-chair and Minister without Portfolio from 2010. She famously attended the first Cabinet meeting in 10 Downing Street dressed in shalwar kameez, the traditional loose trousers and long tunic worn by both men and women in Pakistan.

A handful of British Muslim women may have become more prominent in the past two decades, but how far has the public understanding of them changed?

The identity of the British Muslim woman – as with all women – is unique to the individual. Muslim women are of different races, cultures, ethnicities, shapes and sizes, social and economic backgrounds and educational experiences, and they hold different personal and political convictions, different aspirations and achievements.

We all have a different story to tell. When individual stories are told, they become part of a collective experience, which can shape a different future – and, I hope, shape the present by creating a new understanding.

This is my story. Through my experiences, I will explore and seek answers to controversial questions, from race, culture, integration and terrorism to hair dye and headscarves.

What credentials do I have?

I am a Muslim woman who arrived in this 'rainbow paradise' as a child. I was privileged to have the benefit of an English education that taught me to be self-questioning, outward-facing and unashamed to have ambition. My love of this country and its people – black, white, brown, Chinese, Polish, Muslim, Christian, Hindu and Jewish – has led me to become a campaigner for human rights, a Liberal Democrat councillor and a patriot. I am lifting the veil on the story of my life and I hope that it will provide a compelling, accurate insight into the real world of Muslim women and help to dispel myths and stereotypes. It will show that one can never make judgements based on someone's appearance and that things aren't always as they seem.

PART ONE

DISCOVERING THE VEIL

CHAPTER 1

THE EARLY DAYS

I arrived in London in 1975 and stepped out of the aeroplane into a blustery, cold, rainy day. I was three years old and hated leaving my home and my grandparents in Bangladesh. The tears were cold on my cheeks.

Amma (Mummy) held my hand tightly.

'Don't cry,' she said, and I noticed that her eyes, too, were red from quietly weeping. We were like two water lilies – the Bangladeshi national flower – ripped from a warm pond and cast down in the wet concrete streets of an overcast and brooding city.

My dad had a job as a dockworker in the Chatham Docks in Kent. We moved into a small house in a narrow street of identical houses and were the only family of colour. We were an oddity, vaguely exotic. Nevertheless, we had strong social and family values, much like most other people in our working-class community. My brother, Joynal, would suck his bottle with plump hands and look with dark mischievous eyes framed with thick lashes at other mothers stopping to peer into his pram, while I stared up into the ring of shiny white faces. My mother did not speak English and just smiled and nodded politely when the other women spoke to her.

My mother came from a professional family. Her father and grandfather were businessmen. She always went out in the most elegant saris ordered from India and wore makeup to highlight her high cheekbones and big, dark eyes. She had been a social butterfly in Bangladesh, fluttering through the bazaars with her sisters and friends, while I spent my early years being cared for by my grandmother. In England, Amma lost her sparkle and began to dress in a burqa, the black, ultra-conservative garment she rarely wore in Bangladesh. She was hiding from the world and mourning the life she had left behind.

Over time, the burqa ceased being just a veil to hide behind and became a symbol of her sadness and oppression. It took all of my mother's will to cast it off and take her old saris from the wardrobe in her bedroom; a room with dark curtains and striped wallpaper like bars in a prison. It was difficult for her to adjust to her new life when her first language was not English. She could no longer beckon a rickshaw and take off for afternoon tea and visits with her cousins. She had no female friends or relatives in Rochester, and she was too timid to try and communicate with our generous neighbours, who had explained to Dad where to shop and how to get the bus into the city. My young mother did not find it easy taking care of my hyperactive brother, who could run before he was a year old and talked non-stop in a babble of Bangladeshi and English. I added to her woes by continually asking when I could go home to my grand-parents. We were like fish thrown up on the shore, wriggling hopelessly, trying to get back to the sea.

My father felt honoured to have been granted the right to live in England and to have a well-paid job. He was an open, kind man with smiling eyes. The other men liked him, and he never complained of bigotry, exclusion or cruelty. Some-times another worker called him 'Paki' or 'darkie', as they would call those with red hair 'ginger', or an overweight man 'tubby' or 'fatty'. This has become unacceptable in our po-litically correct times, and rightly so, but in the 1970s these labels were used more through ignorance than prejudice. My dad laboured alongside British workers. He was one of them, drawn into the fold by common experiences in a community that was proudly working-class. We have grown more tolerant but lost that sense of solidarity. 'Them' and 'us' used to be defined as the rich and the poor. Now, more often than not, 'them' and 'us' refers to skin colour and religious persuasion.

It was many years before I understood that my father had torn up his roots in Bangladesh and come to England to build a better life for his family; the motivation of 99 per cent of immigrants. Statistics show that immigrants are good for a country's economy. They work hard and pay more in taxes than they take out in benefits. It's not just monetary impact that they have made, but qualitative social and economic contributions. We only need to look at the number of refugee doctors who work in the NHS, for example. As of May 2020, 13.8 per cent of NHS staff were of non-British nationality, having come to the UK from over 200 other countries, and of these, 5.5 per cent were nationals of other EU countries. Other examples of ways in which the UK has been enriched by immigration include the £5 billion curry industry, the rag trade in east London built by Jewish tailors, and the Ugandan Asian refugees who transformed Leicester after Idi Amin expelled almost 60,000 of them in 1972.

My father was always patient and sweet with my mother. The family and home are central to Bangladeshi life. The kitchen is the female domain which, traditionally, men rarely enter. Not so with my parents. They would chat away together as they made the evening meal, Mum chopping vegetables while Dad prepared the chicken and fish. Fish and rice form the basis of most Bangladeshi dishes, always spiced with curry, chutney, tamarind and coconut. We cleaned our plates and ate samosas and paratha for snacks. It was followed by char – tea – a word borrowed by the English from the Indian subcontinent and usually articulated as 'a nice cup of char'. Dad had adjusted to English life, but his palate remained loyal to Bangladesh.

My mother was content for these few hours every night when the family was together. But the days were long and lonely. One day, I found her sobbing in the bedroom with her face buried in a ball of black material. I quietly crept behind her to see what it was. It was the 'dreaded' burqa that seemed to be associated with sadness and change. A piece of material that had been part of familiar and normal life in Bangladesh, and which had never attracted stares or prejudgement, had now become an item of controversy and misperception, but as a young child I did not immediately make this connection. I didn't say a word. I just sat beside her while she cried, a confused five-year-old trying to make sense of my mother's sorrow. How dare this piece of clothing bring such sadness to my mother and kidnap me from the life I had once had?

I lay in my bed that night and made a plan. Even at the age of five, I thought dealing with a problem through action was better than being passive and hoping it would go away. The next day, while Amma was taking a nap with Joynal, I went to find the burqa with the intention of putting it in the dustbin. It was in a paper bag and the moment I opened it, I was struck by all the scents and sensations of my grandparents' home. The familiar fragrance of Lux soap, the aroma of fresh coconut and the taste of the wind on the days before the monsoon arrived. A feeling of euphoria washed over me. I didn't want to be in England. I wanted to go home. I wanted to be embraced by the unforgettable perfumes of Bangladesh. I wanted to hear my nana's stories again. Fat tears rolled down my cheeks. I held the burqa to my face, just as my mother had done, and it felt as if there was nothing else to hold on to.

This feeling of loss passed suddenly and completely one

Saturday morning when Dad and Mum took me on the bus to town to buy my school uniform, sensible Clarks shoes fastened with a buckle and a blue raincoat with a belt. It was all wrapped in a parcel that Dad carried, and we celebrated by visiting Rochester Castle and going to a tea shop that served pastries on a three-level stand. Joynal was naughty and wouldn't sit still. Amma now had a new babe in arms, my sister Ruksana, and I felt very grown up with my glass of orange juice and the brown paper parcel on the chair beside me.

A few days later, in September 1977, I plunged into the busy, competitive world of first year at St John's Church of England Primary School and settled down immediately. My parents were acutely aware of the importance of education. If life is a race, immigrant children start behind the rest and must work twice as hard if they want to achieve their goals or, better said, the goals set for them by their parents. My father had already begun to teach me to read at home. I was placed in the top group and was partnered with another girl who needed help with her reading. Having this responsibility made me work harder and I came to see that you learn by teaching. My earliest ambition was to be a teacher.

I loved school. I liked being dressed like the other little girls. We were all the same in our uniforms except, of course, I was brown with thick, straight black hair and brown, almond-shaped eyes. Once, a timid little boy, small for his age, had a picture book with a dark-skinned girl wearing a crown and asked me if I was a princess. I like to think I said yes.

Being a good reader and willing to take on any challenge gave me self-confidence, and confidence attracts people to you. Before I started school, I had never noticed that people were different colours. This was first made obvious to me by the *Janet and John* books from which we learned to read. Both Janet and John had blonde hair and blue eyes – like half the children in the class. The headmistress was pale and blonde. Everyone in authority was white, I realised, and from an incredibly early age I longed to see someone like me in a place of power. Two things in the *Janet and John* books struck me as odd. Firstly, Janet and John came from a socioeconomic background far removed from the humble backstreets of Rochester. Secondly, Janet was usually in the kitchen helping her mother, while John was with his father in the garden. These roles didn't make any sense to me because I was always in the garden with my dad and my parents helped each other in the kitchen.

I don't ever recall reading a book with images of people who looked like me, but I was taught from books with people of colour in exaggerated settings. Christopher Columbus was always described to me as one of the greatest explorers of all time; in the books I read he had discovered the 'Red Indians', which is what some of the books I was taught from called Native Americans. When I asked a teacher about this, her explanation was that the Red Indians' skin was slightly redder than that of the Indians in India. As a nine-year-old, I found this confusing and very strange; I took one of the books home and looked in the mirror to assess my skin colour and compare it with the image in the book about Red Indians.

Fascinated by the project on Red Indians and their difference in colour, I even watched John Wayne's Western films, trying to look at the skin tone of the Red Indians portrayed in them. By then, we had a colour television, which assisted my investigations.

It was during the following year, when we studied Pocahontas, that I finally found someone who looked like me. I studied her story as if it were mythical, through the eyes of Captain John Smith, whom she allegedly saved on more than one occasion. Although there have been many conflicting versions of her story, I was mesmerised by the portrayal I read of a powerful, heroic woman.

In the book that we read, Pocahontas (real name Matoaka) was instrumental in maintaining relations between her father, Chief Powhatan, and the Jamestown colonists – the first Europeans to arrive on Powhatan land in what we now know as Virginia. She may have been more privileged than her peers, but she still had to learn 'women's work', and undertook other charitable tasks such as bringing food to the hungry settlers and helping negotiate the release of Powhatan prisoners.

She was initially married to an Indian, Kocoum, in 1610, before being lured onto an English ship in 1613. After being kidnapped by the captain, Samuel Argall, she lived under the care of a minister, Alexander Whitaker, learned to speak English and converted to Christianity. She was baptised and given the name Rebecca. It was during her imprisonment that she met her second husband, John Rolfe, and the couple married in 1614. It is not certain what happened to her first husband, but divorce was permitted in Powhatan culture.

In 1615, Pocahontas gave birth to a son, Thomas, and was revered as a princess when the family travelled to England. Some Londoners even referred to her as 'Lady Rebecca Wolfe'. It was hoped that the marriage would create cohesion between the Indians and the colonists.

In March 1617, Pocahontas, her son and her husband set sail for Virginia, but shortly after departure, Pocahontas became seriously ill and had to return ashore at Gravesend. She died on 21 March 1617, although the true cause of her death still remains a mystery. It is not clear whether she died from a disease or was murdered with poison.

Our class visited the graveyard at St George's Church in Gravesend, Kent, where Pocahontas is thought to be buried, in preparation for our class play on her life.

I was incredibly excited when I was chosen to play the role of Pocahontas. I suppose for the teacher that was a no-brainer, given that I was the only one with long dark hair and brown skin. My parents were excited that I would be playing an Indian princess, but things were not quite as they expected when they turned up for an afternoon showing of the play. My parents sat in the front row with one of my younger sisters, who happily sucked on her bottle.

I wasn't quite dressed in the way that I think my parents imagined their Indian princess should be dressed. I had feathers in my plaited hair, white markings on my face, and I wore a long fawn dress, with a pair of ballet shoes on my feet. As I made my entrance, my mother whispered something to my father, but he seemed to hush her.

John Rolfe was played by my classmate, blond-haired William, who was overly excited to be acting opposite me, although I am not sure that the feeling was mutual. His parents were also happily seated in the front row and they beamed at me all the way through.

In the last act of Pocahontas's final moments, as I lay dying, John Rolfe took my hand and cried. I said goodbye, gently tried to pull my hand away and, out of the corner of my eye, watched my parents – who seemed to show no emotion. William deliberately held onto my hand, pulling it back towards his chest. I tried to snatch it back again, bringing him closer to my face. That wasn't helpful, since my parents' mouths opened in surprise and even my sister stopped sucking her bottle to watch. My heart was beating fast, because William really looked as though he was going to kiss me – and that wasn't in the script. I just wanted the play to end so that I could jump up and whack him with one of my feathered plaits. It was by far the most comical picture imaginable, with the other children giggling in the background and my parents transfixed to their seats with mouths wide open, afraid of what might come next.

Finally, it ended, and William's parents jumped up and said, 'Well done! Superb, Rabina!' My parents looked on,

bewildered; it really wasn't quite the play they had envisaged, with the British Raj nowhere to be found.

Pocahontas's true story is rarely told and differs vastly
from the image that has been portrayed by the Disney clas-
sic. It is important to understand her true legacy, as it relates
to people like me in public life, the challenges we face and
the courage and determination that we need to show in the
face of discrimination and pre-judgement. Nevertheless,
the story has been told and retold so many times that some
details that started as fantasy have become embedded as
truths.

Extensive research conducted by Camilla Townsend,
author of *Pocahontas and the Powhatan Dilemma* and a
professor at Rutgers University, concluded that Pocahontas
was 'braver, stronger and more interesting than the fictional
Pocahontas'.

Pocahontas was favoured by her father because of her per-
sonality and intelligence. She was only about ten years old
when she first met Captain John Smith. After she allegedly
intervened when the Powhatans were ready to beat him with
clubs, she began visiting Jamestown regularly, accompanied
by a group of Powhatan envoys. Her real name, Matoaka,
had been concealed from the colonists for her safety.

Although the Disney film depicts a love story between
Pocahontas and John Smith, this is widely acknowledged to
be historically inaccurate. From what has survived of Smith's
original notes, it is clear that he and Pocahontas spent time

teaching each other basic aspects of their languages, rather than having any romantic involvement, given that she was just a child at the time.

Pocahontas's true story is not only one of conflict, starvation and kidnap but of immense courage and extraordinary strength in the face of immense adversity.

It may seem strange to some as to why Pocahontas played such an important part in my life at primary school, but there was no other role model to whom I could relate. I was always looking for someone like myself, and Pocahontas gave me that at primary school. The white girls did not understand why she was important to me when, for them, Florence Nightingale was even more so. In a classroom discussion, my white peers spoke about how the wonderful Nightingale tended to the wounded in Turkey during the Crimean War. Her night rounds earned her the label 'The Lady with the Lamp'. Among many other achievements, including social reform in healthcare and nursing, Florence Nightingale established the first scientifically based nursing school at St Thomas' Hospital, London, in 1860. She was the first woman to receive the Order of Merit and following her death in 1910 her family were offered a state funeral and burial for her in Westminster Abbey. However, they refused and instead she was honoured with a memorial service at St Paul's Cathedral, London before being buried in Hampshire.

Florence Nightingale has always been regarded as a heroine, and the majority of people will know who she is and what she did. Conversely, although many people will recognise the name Pocahontas, not many will know her true story and the significant role that she played because she was from a culture to which white British people cannot relate. The media has been responsible for portraying images of oppressed Muslim women, rather than powerful images of those who have performed heroic actions to bring about positive change.

When I was growing up, there were no black or Asian dolls apart from the ubiquitous golliwogs made famous by Robertson's jam and marmalade. The company started carrying the little black figure on labels in the 1920s and continued to do so until political correctness prevailed in 2001. When I was at school, children saved jam bottle wrappers to send off for golliwog enamel brooches that five-year-olds believed were realistic representations of black people. There was also a series of Enid Blyton books with golliwogs depicted as simple, sometimes villainous characters. As recently as the 1970s, such books were not seen as racist but, subtly, that's just what they were. They showed dark-skinned people as different, comical or sinister, and this subtext leaves a residue that's hard to scrub away. Perhaps this could be partly attributed to the fact that representation of people of colour in the media was still largely inaccurate and limited. Children learn and develop through repetition and example. When the only people of colour they see are caricature dolls and children's book characters, those dolls and books matter. Actively demonstrating tolerance, fairness and equality leads to what George Orwell called 'common human decency'. Modelling prejudice, discrimination and intolerance leads to bigotry, chauvinism and violence.

The maps on the wall in school in the 1970s had hung there for thirty years and showed the British Empire marked in red – I assume to show that the sun was always rising somewhere as elsewhere it was going down. Most teachers remembered the war, the powerful, patriotic speeches of Winston Churchill, and the great victory over Germany to liberate Europe. While the war had brought people on these islands together like never before, it gave them a foggy view of our history and place in the world. When I progressed from St John's to Troy Town Primary School, history was added to the curriculum and I was surprised, aged nine, when the teacher insisted that Bangladesh was a part of India. Of course, India, Pakistan, Bangladesh and Sri Lanka (still described as Ceylon in our class) were all coloured red on the map and had indeed been one vast region called British India from 1858 to 1947, when the country became independent and was partitioned. Bangladesh only became fully independent in 1971 after fighting a war with West Pakistan in which my mother was lucky to survive an air attack. I knew my history.

I tried to tell the teacher these things, but she believed she had proved the point that India and Bangladesh were the same country by asserting that my mother wore an Indian sari. By that reasoning, if you put on a pair of clogs, you must be Dutch. The next day, she announced that we were going to study the chapter in our book on 'Rabina's home country,

India and Bengal', the latter not a country but a culturally homogenous region divided between India and Bangladesh.

My teacher had studied history at university and time must have stopped for her when she got her degree. She felt safe living in this vision of how life used to be and, surely, should remain. It was a valuable lesson to me, perfectly illustrated by a quote by William Blake I read years later: 'The man who never alters his opinion is like standing water and breeds reptiles of the mind.'

Not all the teachers were the same. Though some were stuck in the past, Miss Davis clearly lived in the present. One day, out of the blue, she told the other children in our Year Five class that they were lucky to have me as a classmate because they could travel across the world just by talking to me about my life and background. Miss Davis was young and open-faced with curly blonde hair. She was also Welsh, so understood a little of what it felt like to be an outsider in England. I felt touched by her words without realising that what she had done was give me the burden of representation; of being a spokesperson for Bangladeshis, Muslims and brown people. What she did was motivated by compassion and a desire for me to feel accepted by my classmates, for which I was grateful, even though the onus was now on me, and not her, to educate my peers on our culture.

She asked me to give a talk on Gandhi. She knew he was Indian, not Bangladeshi, but Gandhi was the most famous person from the subcontinent and instrumental in both independence and partition. Of course, I asked my dad for help, so we went to the library in Rochester that Saturday morning. I read about Mahatma Gandhi in the *Encyclopaedia Britannica* and was ready to give my presentation the following week. It consisted mostly of a potted history of Gandhi's life and how he was universally admired for bringing about a revolution by peaceful means. I added a personal note, telling the class that my paternal grandfather had lived under the British Raj and resented Britain because it had left India after taking advantage of the nation's assets for hundreds of years in a way that led to civil war when Pakistan divided into two distinct areas thousands of miles apart.

There was an awkward silence. Then one of the boys asked me if, as a Muslim girl, my grandfather would have been angry that I didn't wear a black scarf, and would I cover my face soon? The other children leaned forward with wide eyes and open mouths while I thought about my reply.

'My grandmother never covered up in black, so I am sure he wouldn't have asked me to do so.' I paused. 'My mother wears a sari and uses the end of her sari to cover her head. It is a personal choice.'

Miss Davis had done her job. Preparing the presentation had made me research my own past and gave the children in the class the opportunity to think about the world beyond the shores of England. While I got the impression that most of my classmates enjoyed the talk and were supportive of my explanation about veils, I had a feeling that some of the others were less enthusiastic and had views shaped by what was said at home when they had dinner with their parents.

At five, we are little sponges drawing in knowledge from every direction. At age nine we are already growing opinions and prejudices. Children are like computers. If we are programmed at a young age to pre-judge people based on the way they look, we will do so for the rest of our lives.

My grandmother's headscarf, in fact, was similar to that which British women used to tie up their hair when leaving the house in the 1940s, and which remained fashionable among the female cast in the television soap *Coronation Street* as a way to cover their curlers. Like most families, we turned on the TV to follow the convoluted lives of Ena Sharples, Elsie Tanner and Ken Barlow, and I was pleased to see multicultural Britain finally represented in 1983 when Shirley Armitage, played by Lisa Lewis, appeared as the first major black character to move into Coronation Street.

Our neighbours at that time never defined us by religion. We were foreigners, Pakis, Indians, or 'that family from overseas'. But also 'workers', a wheel among all the others on the constantly moving carriage of the community. Just as people might say 'that Irish family', we were 'that dark-skinned family'. This was merely a description, used without malice or preconceptions. I was the 'little girl with curly brown hair' who talked to everyone and was always asking questions. I was invited to all the birthday parties and other little girls loved coming to our house to eat magical sweets made by my mother with ghee, cashew nuts, raisins and syrup. After eating sweet sticky gulab jumans once, you are addicted for life.

It was very traditional to sing Christian hymns at school assemblies, but now some schools no longer do so as they embrace other faiths to reflect the diversity of our country. We also had a music class every Thursday afternoon, and I remember walking over the green slopes of The Vines behind Rochester High Street, kicking the golden leaves and singing 'Autumn Days', my favourite song.

In September, we celebrated Harvest Festival at school. Everyone brought offerings of food that were distributed to elderly people and the poor. The festival falls on the nearest Sunday to the harvest moon and has been practised in England since pagan times. The occasion is similar to Eid, or Eid al-Fitr (the breaking of the fast), which comes at the end of the month-long abstinence of Ramadan. On this day, we wear our best clothes and take a meal shortly after sunrise. Children receive gifts – like Christmas – and alms are given to the poor. We invited our Rochester neighbours to have tea and cakes. One year, two local non-Muslim women who had become good friends of Amma's dressed in her saris and came with us to walk in the park where we called out Happy Eid to other families, making it more a community holiday than purely a Muslim one.

Apart from Mr and Mrs Patel in the Indian takeaway, I rarely saw other Asians. Dad had already introduced my brother and me to the teachings in the Quran but had decided it was time to meet the wider Muslim community by attending the nearest mosque, which was in Gillingham. Most of the worshippers came from Pakistan originally and it was here that I first saw women dressed similarly to the men in shalwar kameez – shalwar being baggy trousers, and kameez a long shirt or tunic – except more colourfully, and with a shawl or matching headscarf. It was all very relaxed, and I recall only once seeing a woman in the mosque veiled in a niqab.

My mother was comfortable in her sari, using the end to cover her head, as is often the custom in south Asia, and never a veil. It was also the convention for girls to cover their heads and I wore a scarf for the first time, not pinned, but loosely thrown over one shoulder. Needless to say, every time the imam was about to pass, my brother Joynal pulled my scarf off.

Rochester has more hills than the Himalayas; not as high, but just as steep. The Bashirs had opened a takeaway on the top of the hill beyond our house before we moved there and I watched from the window as our neighbours set off like Nepalese Sherpas at teatime to climb the hill and return again clutching carrier bags packed with lauki kofta, rogan josh and vindaloo. People were getting their first taste of Asian spices and now, forty years on, curry is Britain's favourite food. Just as we Asians adapt and become a little more English, I like to think the English have adapted too – however unwillingly – and become a little more exotic.

Christmas was coming. Rochester was strung with illuminations. Neighbours erected trees in their front windows with lights that winked on and off. There was heavy snowfall in December 1981 and it turned out to be one of the severest winters ever recorded. At school we kept our coats on in class. We made paper chains and decorations. We sang carols and recited the Lord's Prayer, which was perfectly natural for me. It often comes as a surprise to people to learn that in the Quran, Jesus is a Muslim prophet born to the Virgin Mary – Maryam in Arabic – who is the only woman to have an entire chapter named after her. Adam, Noah and Abraham all have their place in Islamic holy scriptures. The belief in one God is shared by Jews, Christians and Muslims. You don't have to look far below the surface – skin colour, religion, favourite football club – to find that we have far more in common than we are different.

I was thrilled to be cast as the angel Gabriel in the Nativity play. This required wearing a halo that, when we tried it at home that afternoon, kept slipping down. Mum tried without success to make it work and stomped off impatiently to put the rice on to boil. I bit my tongue and waited for my dad to come home. He was a man with immense inner peace and his presence always made me feel calm. Men he worked with would have a 'private word' with Abdul when they had problems with their wives or children, with debts or health, or with their plans to train for a new occupation. Sometimes, when people have complications in their lives, all they need is a sympathetic listener and a few words of support.

Dad had left the docks, after years of putting Vaseline up his nose to prevent him inhaling asbestos, in the absence of appropriate clothing, taking a new job at British Gypsum to make fresh plasterboard and acoustic ceilings. His work was well paid and he made good friends with white men who would stay in contact with him years after. My father was conscious of rising prices and the needs of his growing family. Joynal was now six and had started at the infant school in September. Ruksana was nearly three and Rohima was six weeks old. My youngest sister, Mehera, would be born two years later when I was eleven and ready to start senior school.

As soon as the door opened, I blurted out my problem with the slipping halo and Dad promised to fix it as soon as he had had a bath and eaten. He was a workman in loose, dark overalls, a flat cap and sturdy work boots by day, an Englishman in his shirt and jacket when he went out with his family and a Bangladeshi at night when he changed into his lungi, a traditional cotton sarong worn by Bengali men. He combed back his thinning, wet hair and sat at the head of the table with Rohima on his lap. Now that he worked longer hours, Mum missed the time they had spent together in the kitchen. Dad recited the prayer of thanks for the food we ate before serving himself from the bowl of rice and selection of curries. He ate slowly, pausing to tickle the baby, asking us in turn about our day. For my dad, the evening meal was a meditation, a time for being together as a family. He noticed that I was bolting down my chicken and smiled his ever-knowing smile across the table. 'We will wash the dishes together, Rabina,' he said. 'But first, I know an angel who needs a halo.'

I slowed down. We helped ourselves from the bowl of tangerines and only when the prayer was said at the end of the meal did Dad set about making a wire contraption from old coat hangers that fitted under my arms and supported a halo above my head. I also needed a costume. Mum joined us and we went to look at the clothes in her bedroom. For some reason, I was terrified that she was going to suggest the burqa, long unused and still in the paper bag in the drawer. I need not have worried. Black is not a suitable colour for an angel and Dad produced from the wardrobe the pretty white cotton sari Mum changed into when she read her salah (prayers). Mother said 'No'. I said 'Yes, yes, yes please!' and she relented when Dad told her she could ask her mother to send two new saris from Bangladesh.

Mum always needed encouragement but then quickly got into the spirit of the enterprise. She set about cutting the sari into a new shape and stitching it into a costume that would have made the real angels jealous. Mum had regained her old confidence. Her English had improved and heads turned when she arrived at the school for the Christmas Nativity dressed in her best gold and red sari beneath her coat – brown and exotic among the pallid English winter faces.

The curtains were closed. The lights went down. Mary and Joseph shuffled onto the stage with a swaying donkey composed of two boys. The Wise Men appeared with their gifts of gold, frankincense and myrrh. The shepherds stood in the background; one little girl, dressed as a sheep, gripping a lamb in a stranglehold. I stood in the background, arms outstretched, saying my lines in my head until the last scene when I stepped to the front of the stage to say, 'I bring good tidings. On this day, Mary, the wife of Joseph, will have a son and she shall name her son Jesus.'

People clapped. The cast bowed and I stepped forward beneath my coat hanger halo and said, 'My cloak and costume were made from my mother's sari that she always dresses in to say her prayers.'

There was a moment's polite confusion, and then everyone clapped again, even more loudly.

To this day, I am not sure what prompted me to do this. It just seemed like the right thing to do. My mother had worked for days sewing the sari. Like my father, she had sacrificed her own wellbeing to provide a better life for her children. I would not have been able to articulate this at the time, aged nine, but I felt a pressing desire to let the families enjoying the Nativity play know that we were proud to be part of the community.

It was also the first time that I had shown that I was not afraid to stand on the stage and express my thoughts.

CHAPTER 2

FINDING ME

I found myself by reconciling the varying identities of my life and finding the place where I could be me: comfortable, unafraid and happy. My childhood experiences of searching for myself in a maze of blissful ignorance, odd stereotypes and confrontations remind me that even now, the process of finding 'me' in Britain's green and pleasant pastures will never end.

When I became a teenager, Amma rather hoped that I would start wearing a headscarf, while Abba didn't mind one way or the other. My father was a wise, well-read, modern man who strongly believed that people should make their own choices; that goodness comes from within, not just from following the dictates of custom or religion. People often imagine Muslim men are dictators who order their wives and children about like servants. That may be true in some circumstances, and indeed in any religion, but my father believed in discussing our differences and reaching a

MY HAIR IS PINK UNDER THIS VEIL

compromise. The compromise in this case was that I carried a headscarf, but it was rarely on my head – more likely, it would be found around my waist, over my shoulder or being used to play tug-of-war in the playground.

In the 1980s, ringlets, long, curly locks and big hair were all the rage. I loved Culture Club, The Bangles and Whitney Houston. I wanted big hair like the pop idols we adored. When I told Karen, my best friend, that I wanted a perm, she literally shrieked with joy and went with me to Sharon's Hairdressers, a small two-room salon on the ground floor of a terraced house. I had to spend all my modest savings on booking the hairdo and made an appointment for 2.30 the following day. That meant I had to skip school that afternoon, in order to get home at the usual time, not long after four.

Karen and two other girls decided that we would make a party of it. Armed with crisps and fizzy drinks, we bowled into Sharon's ten minutes early and the girls watched while she began by washing my hair and complaining that, as I had so much of it, the job was going to take longer than she had anticipated.

The smell of ammonia gave me a headache and made my eyes sting. I had to sit for two hours, fretting, with my scalp held in the vice of four dozen curlers. I was obviously going to be late home, so Karen raced off to my house to say that I had been kept behind after school. This was a good excuse. I was often outspoken and no stranger to being punished by being made to write lines during detention. I learned to write fast, a skill that would be useful in the future.

When the curlers finally came out, a stranger looked back at me from the mirror.

'Oh my gawd, you look like that girl from the Tia Maria advert. You know, that dark one?' I looked puzzled as Sharon started her record player and put on the song *After Dark*.

'I know,' Karen said. 'You look like Iman.'

I suppose this was a compliment, although I didn't think so at the time. I felt like Medusa, with a head of venomous curls that I covered with a scarf before I went home, trying to look serene to face my mother. We got through the evening meal, with the family gathered around the table taking turns to talk about their day in between eating plates of curried vegetables and rice. I didn't need to be reminded to do my homework. I was happy to hide my hair in the next room behind an impressive pile of schoolbooks. We went to bed and when Amma came in to make sure we had said our prayers, she looked at me with my vast tied-up nest of hair, covered in a scarf, and I had to kick my sister under the bed-covers to keep her quiet.

My mother finally caught me without a scarf when she insisted on oiling my hair after I'd missed my oil sessions for three weeks running. By the time she saw the perm, I had grown to like the idea that I looked like Iman – Zara Mohamed Abdulmajid, the Somali model who married David Bowie a few years later. Amma screamed. She wasn't well-versed in pop culture and went to the Pakistani mosque to pray for my soul.

When I was a young girl, before I had started school, local Muslims came to our tiny house in Chatham for Friday prayers until my father co-founded the town's first mosque in an end-of-terrace house at the bottom of the hill in the mid-1980s. It was minute compared to the Gillingham Mosque, which I went to aged ten, but a valuable addition that enabled the community to develop a sense of cohesion. Amma always cooked iftar, the meal that breaks your fast at sunset during Ramadan, for everyone. I learned from her how to make samosas by rolling the dough and adding the cooked fillings to make pastry envelopes. Now you can buy ready-made samosas, but I like to do it the old way with my own family.

In the early days, the mosque was damp with limited facilities. Over the years it has improved beyond all recognition. It can now hold Eid events. The elders work with the local council and the space is used for community events. The advancements that this centre has made are representative of the increasing nationwide efforts of mosques to play an active part in the lives of all their worshippers. Today, women's groups all over the country are also playing a more active role in their local mosques. Sometimes, prayers are conducted in English and there are BSL translators so that the needs of people with disabilities can be met. Young imams are beginning to see the mosque as a public building and have introduced libraries, sports facilities and restaurants open to the general public. This is also seen as a way to bring back young Muslims who have strayed from their faith. I can think of no better way for people to mix and assimilate than playing sports together, whether football, cricket or athletics. Is there a better, more beloved example of successful integration than Sir Mo Farah, the 5,000 and 10,000 metre Olympic gold medallist?

My brother and sisters are active members of the Muslim community in Kent, where they organise barbecues, celebrations and fairs open to local people. It is vital that management committees in mosques make sure that the facility is not just a place of worship but a venue where people of all faiths can come together to learn and appreciate the message of peace and goodwill. The word 'Islam' means 'peace'. It is up to all Muslims to live by that word and ensure the message is heard loud and clear.

The message obviously reached one thoughtful person after the terror attacks in Christchurch, New Zealand, in March 2019. My mother told me that someone had left a basket of flowers outside the mosque in Chatham with the message: 'We are sorry for your loss.' When she told me, it brought tears to my eyes as my father, who is no longer with us, would have been deeply touched by such a gesture of friendship.

Like millions of people around the world, I followed the news reports of this shoot-to-kill atrocity by a white supremacist and was impressed by the compassionate response by New Zealand's Prime Minister Jacinda Ardern. She went to the blood-splattered mosque wearing a headscarf to comfort the mourners and openly – and honestly – cried. She offered government funds to pay for all funeral costs, regardless of the victims' immigration status, and immediately pushed through new gun control measures banning military-style assault weapons. How any nation can allow the sale of these weapons, designed not for hunting but the sole purpose of killing people, remains to me a complete and utter mystery; a national madness.

What she did not do was call for a war on terror, or greater surveillance measures, or the repression of civil liberties. When first elected, Ardern did not compete with male politicians by being more masculine than the men, but, on the contrary, created a feminine leadership style that has seen her ratings go off the charts. More importantly, she has shown female politicians across the world that shifting funds from military spending to social welfare programmes, for example, is not only beneficial to the people – it's a vote winner as well.

By affirming in Parliament that she would never utter the name of the perpetrator of the attack in Christchurch, Jacinda Ardern cleverly denied the gunman the celebrity status he was seeking and placed the victims at the heart of the tragedy. By wearing a headscarf – something other non-Muslim women then copied – she showed the Muslim population that they were a welcome and integral part of the community.

Just as some thoughtful person left a basket of flowers outside the mosque in Chatham, I was moved by the news report of Andrew Graystone – the 'man in the flat cap' who stood outside the mosque in Manchester on the day of the Christchurch massacre holding a sign that said, 'You are my friends. I will keep watch while you pray.' A worshipper took a photograph that went viral when it was posted online, receiving thousands of thumbs-up and supportive messages.

That support prompted Andrew Graystone to join Change UK and enter local politics. He told *The Guardian* in May 2019, 'We need to do politics in a different way. I had an enormous response when I stood outside the mosque and, overwhelmingly, what I was hearing was: "We want to build positive relationships and friendships." It feels like our old politics hasn't managed to deliver that.'

Graystone's gesture had been motivated by a sense of Christian fellowship. He had grown tired of politicians losing sight of the bread-and-butter issues: poverty, schooling, health and local services, which, when neglected, create a vacuum that draws in hard-right populists with agendas of fear and division. 'It's the politics of the clenched fist rather than the open hand. I think it's time for the politics of the open hand,' he said.

● ● ●

My mother's generation found it hard to find their place in British society. But they tried, and they were successful in opening the door for their children, the second generation.

Of all the subjects I learned at school, my mother took the

most interest in Home Economics and Textiles, the arts of cooking and needlework. One time, my needlework teacher asked me to bring in a sari and talk about how they are made and worn. Mum helped me to prepare for the lesson and, as was her way, went over the top by packing a suitcase with saris and writing notes in her less-than-perfect English about the materials and traditions. I had intended to take two saris into school and ended up with fifteen.

With the exception of my friend Karen and a couple of other classmates who had visited my home and played dress-up, most of the girls thought the long strips of material were designed to be wrapped around the head. I felt slightly irritated by them. How stupid could they be to not recognise such beautiful pieces of clothing; seven yards of delicate artwork to wrap around the body?

Of course, it wasn't their fault that the sari was an alien object and, as it turned out, it was a wonderful opportunity to share my life by sharing this exotic glimpse of the East. When I showed them how to transform one uncut length of material into a graceful dress full of shimmer and mystery, they were fascinated and couldn't wait to try it themselves. The sari – shari in Bangladesh – is worn with pleats. It is first wrapped around the waist anti-clockwise over a sari petticoat, fastened, then turned and wrapped again around the body in the opposite direction, tucking pleats in the middle. The loose end is left long enough that it falls over the left shoulder with enough material to cover the head when at prayer, or when modesty or allure is called for.

The girls in my class came in different shapes and sizes, tall and short, skinny and plump. They discovered, as I helped them dress, that the sari fits every contour and gives the wearer elegance and femininity. I had enough saris in the suitcase for our teacher to dress in one as well and we all paraded down the corridor, around the playground and back into class. That year, at Christmas, when there was a school party, *five* of the girls came to my house to ask if they could borrow a sari. Big things like integration and cohesion will be accomplished by the small things we can do along the way.

It slowly dawned on me that being different from the other girls had lots of advantages. I discovered that being able to speak a different language was a gift, not a burden. Bengali was not a language that British children learned in school like French or German, and with the gift of two languages, it is easier to learn a third. I felt British, Bangladeshi and European, and couldn't wait to travel the Continent, as my teacher called Europe.

My life with my family was like any other family's: squabbles, laughter, sharing chores and looking out for each other. My only brother, Joynal, is four years younger than me and had learned by the age of seven to strike a hard bargain. During Eid that year, I wore a new maroon and black shalwar kameez. I was given a tray of food as a gift for another Bangladeshi family nearby and was instructed by Amma to observe the tradition at this important religious festival by wearing the dupatta, a shawl-like scarf, over my head. That particular day, my hair was so wonderfully straight and shiny that I slipped the dupatta off accidentally-on-purpose the moment I turned the corner. Two minutes later, I ran into Joynal, aged nine, on his way back from Eid prayers, looking very grown up in his white tunic. He feigned horror and said he would have to inform Mum that I had disrespected her on Eid. I hurried away, but he followed.

'Would you just go home, you brat?' I said through clenched teeth.

Joynal laughed. 'It's going to cost you.'

'You are such a brat.'

'The price goes up now.'

'Such a Del Boy.'

He held out his hand and I had to bribe him with a bag of cola cubes, several rhubarb custards and the promise of my share of the feast day mangoes. And it still didn't stop him from snatching a couple of samosas before he ran off.

It wasn't my day. The next moment, I saw my uncle coming down the street and had to put the tray down in order to drape a bit of the scarf over my head before he saw me. No sooner had I survived that hurdle than I bumped into Anthony and Jamie, two classmates who lived on my street.

'Rabina, what's that on your head?' Anthony asked.

'Are you going to a fancy-dress party?' added Jamie.

They thought they were so funny. I took a long breath that turned into a sigh. I really just wanted to enjoy Eid, as my cousins were coming from London and we were going to take photos and dabble in makeup and other girlie things. I was about to continue my mission when Jamie said:

'Are you getting married, Rabina?'

'I'm twelve years old, do I look old enough to get married?' I screamed back.

They rolled about laughing. Finally, I joined in. We had been friends since primary school. I knew Jamie really liked me and he seemed to prove it when he said, 'The question is, who's gonna want to marry you, Rabina, with that gob of yours?'

My uncle must have heard the fresh screech of laughter and turned back just in time to hear Anthony say, 'I'll marry you, Rabina,' before going down romantically on one knee.

I saw the look of horror on my uncle's face and wanted the ground to open up and swallow me. He happened to be the first imam of the mosque my father had helped found. Like my father, however, he was a practical man, aware that growing up in Chatham was never going to be the same as growing up in Bangladesh. He saw the boys were only having fun and insisted that I share the Eid samosas with them. They gobbled them down.

'Happy Eid, Rabina.'

'Happy Eid.'

Anthony and Jamie ran off with crumbs on their jackets. By this time, the tray was half empty and I walked home with my uncle to get a fresh batch.

'So you have found a husband, Rabina,' he said, and I went bright red.

'No, Uncle. I'm never going to get married.'

'They are friends from your class?' he asked, and I nodded. 'How are you getting on at school?'

'I love school. I want to be a schoolteacher when I grow up.'

'That is a very noble profession. You must work hard and pass all the exams.'

'Don't worry, I'm going to,' I replied.

He thought about that before nodding his head slowly up and down. 'Yes, I think you will.'

Mum was more than a little surprised when I arrived home with a half-empty tray of cold samosas, but my uncle explained that we had shared them with the local people on the way. She noticed that my dupatta was properly draped on my head and happily filled the tray again with fresh offerings.

Eid passed happily, as Eid should, with presents and family, and I understood for the first time why the dupatta, the headscarf, was important as a custom and as a symbol of devotion through prayer, when previously I had thought that the most essential factor was my strong, internal faith. And though I knew now that the veil was important, I really didn't want to wear it to school or to where non-Muslim people were, as I feared judgement and the lengthy explanations that were often required. As with anyone choosing what to wear for a particular occasion, I chose to wear the veil where I felt it was appropriate to do so. We all adapt

according to the situation and wear attire that we don't necessarily like or feel comfortable wearing. Men are expected
to wear suits to formal business meetings, weddings and fu-
nerals, and women will be expected to wear smart, respect-
able outfits, even if they would choose something entirely
different if they had the option.

It is also about religious identity and self-expression. My
father had said that belief was internal, not just an exterior
display of a material object or show of piety. God or Allah
is not just in the clothes you wear, and in the mosque or
church, but inside you and your intentions.

Another holiday I enjoyed was Easter, as it was another opportunity to show goodwill towards our neighbours
when my class went to Rochester Cathedral for the Easter
sermon and to visit the elderly people's homes with baskets
of food. Amma told me I should wear my headscarf to show
respect to my faith and, at Easter, I always obeyed her. My
friends donated tins of baked beans, soups, loaves of bread.
My basket was loaded with portions of chicken biryani and
I noticed when I joined the congregation that strangers
always wanted to sit close to me. The exotic tang of spice and
saffron filled the air and overpowered the harvest aromas of
wheat and barley and vegetables decorating the altar.

Anthony, who had got a taste for Bangladeshi food after
eating Mum's samosas, wanted to buy my donation of chick-
en biryani, and Jamie had the bright idea of going into business. It just so happened that, after Easter, I was desperate

to raise money to buy the new Wham! record and, seizing Jamie's suggestion, I went into competition with the school sweet shop selling containers of chicken biryani.

It was a lesson that I was not cut out for a life in business. The older children who ran the school sweet shop had a monopoly and wanted to keep it that way. One boy pushed my containers of fresh food on the floor and Jamie butted him from behind and shoved him to the floor. They had a big fight, shouting and throwing fists, and by the time they were pulled off each other, they were covered in chicken biryani and there was nothing left to sell.

I had known Jamie and Anthony for a long time. They accepted me as I was, as I accepted them. Sometimes I wore a headscarf – like to visit the cathedral – sometimes I didn't.

Religion is like a pendulum swinging from one extreme to the other. The challenge is finding the balance so that we live in harmony. There are Muslim terrorists – as there are terrorists of every stripe and colour – but they are a minute fraction of the Muslim population. Not 1 per cent, but a fraction of 1 per cent. Muslims fear and condemn them in the same way as the rest of the population do, and more Muslims have died at the hands of the terrorists than any other community.

In 1987, when Margaret Thatcher had been re-elected as Prime Minister for a record third term, the miners had lost their fight to keep the pits open. Other traditional industries were closing down without explanation or alternatives. The Archbishop of Canterbury's envoy, Terry Waite, had been kidnapped by extremists in Lebanon. There was rage and racism in the air. Muslim women were being spat at and having their scarves pulled off on buses and trains – it's always the women that get picked on – and after years of living harmoniously with the neighbours, we had a strange and unexpected confrontation.

I was in the garden helping my sister Ruksana with her homework and keeping an eye on Joynal. He was growing his hair long so that it flicked up at the ends. He was being a nuisance, as always, and I threatened him in Bengali that I was going to tell Mum that he needed a haircut. We were still arguing when I felt a fiery prickle like a bee sting on my neck. Ruksana suddenly screamed.

'Ouch,' she cried.

Then I got another sting on my arm. I stood and saw the neighbour's son, a man of twenty, leaning over the fence. He seemed to have a handful of cigarette butts that he was lighting and flicking at us. Ruksana stood behind me crying.

'Why are you doing that?' I shouted.

He just grinned. It was my brother who came to the rescue. Joynal had a few days before captured a grass snake that he kept in a bottle with the intention of terrifying me and my sisters. My parents by this time had heard Ruksana screaming. They came running out into the garden to find their son wielding the snake in a bottle, the six-foot-tall white giant standing back and his father observing the scene from the upstairs bedroom window.

Amma really lost her temper. She wagged her finger like a

sword and shouted in Bengali. Her scarf fell off and her hair escaped in a luxuriant, well-oiled shower from her bun.

My father waved to the man in the window. He left the garden once the fracas was over and went to talk with his neighbour. We had always had a good relationship with the family and Abba intended to make sure it continued. Was he weak in doing this? No. He was strong. He knew how to turn the other cheek. He knew that the young man next door had lost his job, was looking for someone to blame and chose the 'Pakis' because we were useful scapegoats.

Joynal was praised as the hero of the day and I didn't tell Mum he needed a haircut. What happened to the grass snake, I can't remember.

When there are economic problems, there is an uptick in low-level racist attacks, more often verbal than physical, and it unravels in a chain reaction from politicians to the right-wing press, to working people, into communities and schools.

I remember very well that February in 1990 when I was doing my A-levels and Nelson Mandela had finally been released from prison. He was on the TV news, his then wife Winnie at his side, as he was about to address the huge crowd waiting for him in Cape Town. He said: 'We have waited too long for our freedom. We can no longer wait. Now is the time to intensify the struggle on all fronts. To relax our efforts now would be a mistake which generations to come will not be able to forgive ... Our march to freedom is irreversible.'

This had a profound effect on me. It made me realise that the struggle for equality and acceptance is never won. There are always forces that will try to reverse the gains that ordinary people make. We had a debate on this in school the next day and one boy, Chris, quoting his father, I'm sure, insisted that releasing Mandela would lead to race riots: black against white.

'That's just nonsense,' I said. 'Why should it?'

'Because they're not the same as us, are they? You know, black people?'

'Like me.'

'I didn't say that; you did. All the races are different. They shouldn't get mixed up.'

Karen had told me the things Chris had said behind my back, and this was not the first time we had clashed in the sociology class. He had a habit of making assumptions, like the time when he asked me, 'Your dad owns the corner shop, doesn't he?'

I ignored him and he said, 'It's all right, we know that you lot own corner shops and sell curry powder.'

It was these belittling stereotypical remarks, designed to get a response, that would turn hurt into anger and spark fury when pushed to the limit. So what if people from south Asian backgrounds owned corner shops; what was wrong with that? They were earning a livelihood, not looking for handouts. Years later, when I moved to the East End, I learned that a neighbourhood would not be a community without a corner shop, a post office and a pub.

I knew as I spoke that I was heading for a detention.

'Sometimes you should try and shut the fuck up,' I said. The room became completely silent. You could have heard a paper hanky drop. 'My father does not own a corner shop, as you well know, and my name isn't Patel. And even if it was, so what? As you know, I am not a Paki. I'm from Bangladesh, and you should put your brain in gear before letting your mouth motor off.'

The bell went. The class was over and Mr Edmondson, the teacher, told me to remain behind. He closed the door when the class emptied, and I wondered how many lines I was going to have to write this time.

'I don't disagree with anything you said except for one word,' he told me. 'You will not win debates using swear words. Hone your debating skills and beat the racists by being cleverer than them. Well done.'

I walked home with Karen.

'You were great. That bloody Chris is a real prick,' she said, and it made me laugh.

I turned and asked her: 'Do you see me as different from the other girls?'

'Course you are. You're smarter.'

She stopped and gripped both my arms. It gave me a warm feeling inside and made me really happy. After dinner, I told Abba what had happened that day in class.

'Always stick up for yourself. The only way to fight bullies is to try and reason with them and remember that bullies have often been bullied themselves. You must be kind to them.'

I had been incredibly angry with Chris and some of the other boys, with the bus driver who slammed the door in my face, with the neighbour flicking cigarette butts over the garden fence. My instinct had been to plot some kind of revenge. But my father taught me that it is better to build bridges and that's what I decided to do.

CHAPTER 3

THE CHOICE

For my mother's generation, the rules on headscarves, as with most other customs, were more straightforward. Generally, they did what their fathers and husbands instructed. The contemporary Muslim woman in Europe, out in the workplace and contributing to our evolving society, is more aware of choreographing a course through the world without losing a sense of culture and tradition or, more importantly, herself.

What has not changed is the irresistible role that hair plays in the lives of women. All women. Covered or floating free, coloured pink or au naturel, hair is a fundamental part of our being and femininity. We comb, brush, style, dye, curl and cry over our hair. We treat it with conditioners and precious oils. A bad hair day is a bad day. In the Quran, the word 'hijab' refers to the curtain separating visitors to the Prophet's house from his wives' quarters. The use of the hijab can be read literally or metaphorically; a personal choice more than a mandate.

I made the decision to wear the hijab consistently in my mid-twenties. Like most choices, there was a journey to that point; overcoming bends and bumps, self-questioning, tears and humour, love and loss. But, in the end, I made my choice. The time was right and I knew that allowing my fear of judgement to dictate my decision would be compromising who I was and how I felt. The headscarf is right for me. It is part of my faith and a gift. It is who I am. I feel lucky to have grown up and to have been educated in England. I was determined to serve, to contribute and to put something back into the country and the people who had nourished and embraced me. And I wanted to do so as a British Muslim woman, proud of who I am. I want people to see and understand that in our modern, multi-ethnic, rich and diverse nation, the headscarf is not a barrier between us; it is simply a part of my heritage, as a Scotsman wearing a kilt is a part of his and a Jewish woman wearing a wig is part of hers.

Wearing the headscarf has nothing to do with my family, my father, my brother or the imam at the mosque. I have never been forced to wear a scarf or hijab and I am not and have never been repressed, stifled or subjugated. The purpose of the hijab is modesty. It is not a symbol of male authority, as many Westerners seem to believe. The scarf enriches me, but it doesn't change who I am.

Lady Godiva wore her hair so long that she was able to

conceal herself when she rode naked through the streets of Coventry to protest unfair taxes on the poor. We all know that while the townspeople lowered their eyes, Peeping Tom stole an illicit glimpse from his window. But what is less frequently remembered is that Lady Godiva's protest was against her own husband imposing those new taxes. She was a prototype liberal feminist who enjoyed having long hair.

French women who collaborated with the occupying German forces in the Second World War had their heads shaven as a punishment, observing most likely the verse in 1 Corinthians that says: 'and every woman who prays or prophesies with her head uncovered dishonours her head; for she is one and the same with her whose head is shaven'. The negative implication of a woman with a bare head is apparent and just as convoluted in the New Testament as it is in the Quran. The Ancient Greeks called hair 'the cheapest adornment' but kept slaves, if they were rich enough, to look after it. Michelle Obama told reporters she dealt with her midlife crisis by cutting herself a fringe. In the prize-winning TV series *Fleabag*, the protagonist's sister Claire appears with a terrible haircut and Phoebe Waller-Bridge's character storms in to confront Anthony, the hairdresser. 'Hair is everything!' she screams. 'We wish it wasn't, so we could actually think about something else occasionally, but it is.'

Every generation has its own hair story. It certainly did in my house. My sister Mehera is ten years younger than me and was at college when she looked in the mirror one day and thought to herself: 'I'm really fed up with my hair.' Perms were no longer in fashion. Mehera decided to have lowlights (the opposite of highlights), a process where you darken strands of your hair and create a contrast with various complementary hues. It gives the hair the appearance of more body and a shiny 'wow' effect.

Our grandmother from Bangladesh was staying at the time. Nanu was very observant in every meaning of the word; attentive to her devotions and eagle-eyed when she wasn't at prayer. She wore a spotless, white, starched cotton sari and had the kindly, slightly disapproving look of Gandhi. When Mehera arrived home from the hairdresser wearing an old black headscarf that belonged to me, Nanu rose regally from where she had been sitting and clapped her thin hands together.

'We know what you've been up to. You're on that television programme you and your sisters watch.'

'You have become a secret actress,' Amma added.

'And a model,' said Nanu in a dark whisper.

'What are you talking about?'

Nanu had slowly crossed the room and she whipped the black headscarf from my sister's head. 'There!' she said, like a magician producing a rabbit from a hat.

Mehera shook her head of elegant lowlights and my mother immediately got on the phone to call me at the Peabody Housing Association, where I worked as a consultant in a big open office filled with staff. I wasn't exactly sure why she had made this call; either I was considered in some way responsible for my sister's transgression, or Amma wanted me to join them in condemning her new career choice.

'Mehera is on television,' she cried in a voice so loud everyone in the office stopped what they were doing.

'On television?' I said dubiously.

'She's an actress. An actress. And a model. She's done it behind our backs. What are we going to do?'

'Are you sure?'

'We have the proof.'

Nanu must have grabbed the phone from her. 'Proof,' she repeated. 'We have seen her.'

'On television?'

'In a magazine.'

The phone was slammed down and I held up my palms as if in surrender.

'Wrong number. A couple of mad people,' I explained to my colleagues.

I pieced together the full story when I arrived home. Mehera had indeed spent the afternoon at the hairdresser's and made her entrance in the black headscarf to hide her hair, not because she had suddenly become more pious. For the two amateur detectives, the large round sunglasses added to the scarf was the final confirmation that they were harbouring a clandestine superstar.

'I've been watching you all this time. You are on that programme you giggle at with your sisters. We know what you are up to.'

With great drama, like a lawyer in court, Amma produced

the incontrovertible proof: the magazine with photographic evidence.

Mehera shook her head. 'Amma, please. Look closely. That's not me, it's Katie Holmes from *Dawson's Creek*.'

'What is this Dawson Creek?' demanded Nanu.

'It's a television show in America.' She pointed at the picture. 'That is not me. Katie Holmes is American.'

'No, no, no, no, no,' Nanu tutted, her head wobbling from side to side. 'Is you, Mehera.'

'I wish,' she said.

The two brilliant detectives looked a bit sheepish at having been caught in their hasty assumptions, but the lowlights still had to be dealt with. My father must have heard the commotion and listened outside the door. He entered with his jolly smile.

'Hello, are you having a party?' he asked.

'Your daughter has put lights in her hair, that's what's going on,' my mother answered.

'Oh, that, of course. It was my suggestion.'

'What? You!' she exclaimed. 'I haven't been looking after your daughter's hair all these years for her to go and lose it when she gets old.'

'I saw a picture of an actress in a magazine and I thought Mehera looked just like her.'

Nanu had clasped her hands together to pray.

Father was smiling. My mother was livid. 'Well, now you can tell her to get it back to the right colour,' she said. 'And she needs to have oil every day.'

'Every day,' added Nanu, like it was the end of a prayer.

When I was a small girl in Bangladesh, Nanu combed my hair three times a day to make sure I had not caught lice from the village children. She would then rub in a generous measure of coconut oil. Amma had carried on the tradition in England. She would plait my hair in braids tied with pink ribbons and dress me in bright floral dresses from C&A. In Rochester in the winter when girls were dressed in navy-blue coats and woolly hats, I must have looked like a tropical fruit salad running up the hill to the Indian takeaway.

I had been so brainwashed by my mother and grandmother to believe that hair needs to be kept healthy and beautiful with oil that when my daughter coloured her hair, I had to bite my tongue and remind myself that I had gone through the exact same experiments. The line connecting my perm at fourteen, Mehera's lowlights and my daughter's first sortie with the hair dye is the desire for self-expression, for testing boundaries, for being naughty and, at the same time, feeling that we are finding ourselves. Each generation has different experiences and expectations in a constantly changing Britain that shapes Muslim culture, just as Muslim traditions and styles likewise have an effect on British culture.

Mumzy Stranger (Muhammad Mumith Ahmed) is an award-winning record producer, writer, singer and musician. Mumzy is of Bangladeshi origin and was raised in a traditional Bengali Islamic home in Plaistow, east London. Despite his music not being supported by most of his family, except his mother, he continued experimenting with various MC styles while furthering his academic studies and achieving a BA Honours at the University of Westminster. His initial demo tape was shortlisted for the finals at the BBC Asian network 'Unsung' competition and was then spotted by Rishi Rich who saw his potential. Menhaj Huda is a Bangladeshi-born British film and television director, producer and screenwriter, best known for the controversial movie *Kidulthood*, set among the gangs and hip-hop clubs of west London. He gained a scholarship to study Engineering at Oxford University and after graduating he worked for Sky TV and trained as an editor. By the age of twenty-six, he had launched his directing career. Amina Khayyam is a Bangladeshi-born British dancer, choreographer and dance teacher at the University of Surrey. In 2007, she established the Amina Khayyam Dance Company. Kaniz Ali is a Bangladeshi-born British makeup artist, perfume expert and beauty columnist. She has won numerous awards and styled many celebrities in addition to founding the Kanizmakeup Training Academy in London. She is also a humanitarian aid worker who has helped on projects that provide emergency aid in war-torn countries.

These are just a few examples of successful figures who have influenced British culture and inspired and connected with a generation of young people from all backgrounds. Menhaj Huda's film *Kidulthood*, for example, resonated with young people who felt underrepresented or misunderstood for a variety of reasons, not just race, and also showed the sometimes tragic consequences of one's actions.

Bangladeshi, Indian and Pakistani designers have gone mainstream, adapting Asian fashions to Western tastes, and few young women today are strangers to mehndi (henna) for hair and skin ornamentation. When I was growing up, we never saw a halal fried chicken wing or burger. Today, halal meat can be found in most major UK supermarkets and in fast food chains such as Nando's, Subway and KFC. Add to that the individual halal stores and restaurants, and the UK halal market is worth over £3.3 billion. My halal butcher in east London serves just as many English customers as Muslim.

In sharing these islands of Britain, we are related by common dreams and hopes for the future. In Tower Hamlets, where I work as a local councillor, the needs of poor Bangladeshi, Somali and English families are the same. Their first concern is having decent housing, schools and opportunities for their children. Whatever the far-right and populist politicians try to tell us, we are more similar than different and, in my experience, share the same desires for fair play and common human decency. Imam Ali, the Prophet's son-in-law, one of Islam's first caliphs, or leaders, is fabled to have said, 'People are of two types in relation to you: either your brother in Islam or your brother in humanity.'

Muslims have often been accused of being too conservative, with justification. We have been slow in making changes but now, with the third British Muslim generation coming of age, the wheels are turning faster. According to an Ipsos MORI poll on Muslim social attitudes from May

2018, UK Muslims are becoming more liberal without becoming less religious. It revealed that up to 79 per cent of young Muslims – aged sixteen to twenty-nine – want to be fully integrated in all aspects of British life. They have ethnically diverse friendship groups and believe it is correct that homosexuality is legal in Britain. Young Muslims do not see the choice as being either more British by becoming less Muslim or being more Muslim by becoming less British. According to the poll, they are finding ways to reconcile the two.

Similarly, there are ways in which Muslim women can reconcile the modesty encouraged by their faith with their personal femininity. I wear the hijab but that does not prevent me from being and feeling feminine. I like pretty things – perfume, clothes, shoes, accessories. My mother always took pride in dressing her daughters in delicate attire on Eid days and this certainly influenced the way I like to dress. I didn't use a head covering as an adolescent, except when I prayed and during religious festivals.

When I visited Bangladesh at age thirteen, I never wore a scarf and neither did my cousins, who, I discovered, were far more fashion-conscious than me. Wearing the veil was called 'modern modesty'. It was considered a form of showing off, of putting on an appearance of piety, perhaps to hide less admirable qualities, and was more of a preoccupation with Muslim women in Europe who did not want to forget their cultural and religious roots. My cousins usually wore shalwar kameez or a sari, with the dupatta on one side, which is always flattering.

In Bangladesh, I had more freedom than I had ever had at home in England. With the excuse that I was being 'culturally educated', I was taken off in a rickshaw to the bazaars and tea houses for gossip and 'people watching'. For my older cousins, that meant 'boy watching'. I stayed overnight with distant relatives and was fed a non-stop supply of marzipan syrup to shut me up when I asked too many questions. I enjoyed the holiday, but it never occurred to me that I might want to live in Bangladesh. I felt like a foreigner, a tourist. England was my home.

Another aspect of my education was in the hands of my paternal grandfather. He had lived under the British Raj and saw the colonial era as a time of subjugation for the indigenous people and the exploitation of the country's natural resources. This facet of Bangladeshi history – shared with Pakistan and India – was not taught at school in England and he made sure I went home with these historical blanks filled in.

Grandfather kept a firm hold on his memories because he had suffered more than his fair share of personal tragedy. Shortly before he married Nanu, he had lost six brothers to cholera and she became his heart and his soul, the lifeline he clung to. Nanu was a small, delicate woman who wore fine saris that shimmered in the afternoon light as if she were a butterfly hovering just above the ground. He liked to watch her as she moved around the room and they would always sit close together when he ate his meals.

It would be difficult to find a more loving relationship, although, having said that, my own parents had the same affinity – an unbreakable bond. Like my grandfather watching Nanu, I had seen in my father's eyes the same deep and abiding love across the dining room table when Amma talked about her day. Their marriages had been arranged by their families, of course, as is the custom, and I grew up knowing that the time would come when I would be presented to my husband-to-be.

This event took place when I was nineteen. We sat in the living room with our two sets of parents, looking slightly nervous. My father knew me well enough to know that if I took an instant dislike to this man they had found, there was no way he would be able to drag me down the aisle. He had taught me to be a free thinker, to make up my own mind, to do the right thing and stick to my guns – valuable advice for a politician in any age, but now, in the age of fake news and hyperbole, more so than ever. My father once said to me: 'The world only stays in balance when good people do what's right.' I have never forgotten that.

There was a pot of tea on the table and a plate of pastries that nobody was inclined to eat. The sun slipped through the curtains and lit the side of Aminur's face. I studied him across the room. He was nicely though modestly dressed in a charcoal-grey suit and an open-necked shirt. I thought: 'Well, he's quite handsome. I do hope he knows he's not taking on a submissive woman who plans to sit at home sewing saris and mixing the curry.'

My place, as a second-generation immigrant, was not in the home. It was out in the world. At nineteen, I still intended to become a teacher and had ideas to reform the entire education system: smaller classes, a generous increase in teachers' wages, a more flexible curriculum. I felt, as I do now, that the majority of society's problems can be alleviated if we start in primary school. A good education system will save millions – billions – for the NHS, in skills shortages, in social services and prison. Education for four- and five-year-olds should include diet, teeth cleaning, table manners and common courtesy. If you can press ideas into the heads of little ones when they first start school, they will be better equipped to survive in a constantly changing workspace and more able to contribute to their community. Governments that cut education budgets and pre-school spending are not saving money but creating greater costs in the future.

I poured tea and passed out the pastries. We spoke in Bengali and I could see he had a nice smile and listened politely. I did have my doubts about marrying this stranger with his polished shoes and freshly shaved cheeks. I am sure Aminur felt uncertain too.

A successful arranged marriage is a bit like a blind date that works out. It is terrifying but exciting, like jumping from a plane without knowing if the parachute is going to open when you pull the cord. It is a commitment to something bigger than yourself, than your individual ego. Your vows are seeds that you plant, and it is up to you and your partner to water those seeds and make them grow. An arranged marriage works because you begin with the mindset of wanting to make it work; a bond between two individuals and their families. Surprising as it may seem, arranged marriages have a better record of lasting than those that spring from the first kiss on prom night. Statistics show that although divorce rates vary from nation to nation, love marriages in general break up faster than arranged marriages worldwide. Harvard academic Dr Robert Epstein studied the subject of arranged marriages for eight years, looking at the approaches taken in cultural groups including Indian, Pakistani and Orthodox Jewish communities. He found that within ten years, the connection felt by those in arranged marriages is said to be around twice as strong and that the sense of commitment is very powerful. Another report in *Psychology Today* suggested that there are four main factors. Firstly, as prospective partners are pre-screened, this leaves a small and manageable choice set. Secondly, the problem faced outside these groups of how many partners to date before marrying someone is solved when a marriage is arranged. Thirdly, prospective partners also share many of the same characteristics, which bodes well for a successful union. Finally, arranged marriages encourage one to trust one's gut feelings about the partner, which in turn may lead to more satisfying outcomes.

Just because I agreed to an arranged marriage does not mean that my children's generation will make the same choices as I did. Their choices will be shaped by their circumstances, influences and opportunities in a fast-changing world, just as my choices were.

As poets and songwriters are constantly reminding us, love is a mysterious thing, and it has just as much chance of growing between two people who don't know each other as a couple who have known each other for a long time. It is like climbing a mountain. There may be many paths, but there is only one peak.

An agreement was made. Palms were pressed together in handshakes. Mothers mopped their damp eyes. I was engaged and briefly became the centre of attention among my older female relatives with their wise and worldly experience. My father's younger sister took on the role of my guide. She warned me that I would be expected to obey my husband, to be modest and devoted. 'No more of this running around with your hair flying about, Rabina. When you're married, you'll need to pop the scarf on. Not too tight, just around the hair.'

Little did she know that I was marrying a man who liked to see my hair uncovered and who loved to sing all the Bollywood hits.

I started wearing the tail end of my sari partially covering my hair in front of elders, the sign of respect expected from a new bride. It is tradition for newlyweds to receive invitations to dinner so that you meet each other's friends and family and we received many. Sometimes, at these gatherings of a dozen or so people sitting around a big table, I would suddenly feel my dupatta slipping from its place and Aminur would whisper, 'It's okay, they're my friends.' He was showing off his new wife.

Twenty-eight years later, with all the ups and downs of life in contemporary Britain, we remain a happy team with three children.

Aminur had come to the UK from Bangladesh when he was twenty-three. He had been brought up in a modern environment with all his sisters attending school and college. His mother had been a primary school teacher before she got married and was educated far beyond the level of most women of her generation.

I became a dutiful daughter-in-law in almost every respect. My new sister-in-law (Aminur's brother's wife) and I formed a common front in that we did not wear scarves at weddings and social events except when a nosy aunty appeared with a cross look on her face and a 'tut, tut, tut' on her lips. Both our husbands were mature and wanted their young wives to feel free to make their own choices – as is right and proper, but still new to our rapidly evolving culture. In fact, the mixture of religion and modernity can be confusing. I have one brother-in-law who insists that a woman must wear a niqab, a veil that covers her face except for the eyes, at all times, while his mother believes he should 'loosen up' and that women should be left to make their own choices.

After my marriage, my mother invited the two families to a post-wedding feast. When I arrived at the house, my cousins, even the young ones, had their hair covered by order of the aunties. They complained bitterly when I arrived and wasn't wearing a scarf and, one after the other, the scarves fell away. At nineteen I did not cover my hair with a hijab. At twenty-five I embarked on a journey of a lifetime.

I was working then for City Challenge on the first women-only training course to become a lifeguard. I was cold all the time and had got into the habit of wearing a headscarf when I wasn't in the water, simply for warmth.

When I discovered I was pregnant, it was assumed that I was healthy and I did miss a couple of sessions with the midwife. I didn't have a large bump and in the later stages of my pregnancy, I started to get terrible headaches. When my temperature soared, Aminur took me to my mother and she called the doctor.

Shortly after, I was admitted to the maternity ward at the London Hospital. I gave birth to my daughter, Zakia, with my husband holding my hand. My vision was blurred and I felt so ill that I thought I was going to die. Only then was it discovered that I was suffering from pre-eclampsia, a condition entailing high blood pressure and an excess of protein in the urine that affects some women during pregnancy, which I had never even heard of at the time, and which hospital checks had failed to discover. I prayed that I would live to bring up my child. When I survived and grew strong, I wanted to give thanks, and this was yet another reason why the hijab now seemed right for me. I have worn one ever since.

In Italy, they say that 'clothes maketh the man'. I rather prefer the English saying that 'manners maketh the man', but I can understand the Italian version. Clothes reveal a great deal about who we are. What we wear affects the way people perceive us and how they treat us. When I first started wearing the hijab, I felt as if I had grown from being a girl into a woman. I felt that I was treated with greater respect and it gave me the confidence to enter politics and fight for the rights of my community – *not* the Muslim community; my entire community, for my English and Somali and Polish friends and neighbours; for children suffering neglect and bad treatment, nearly always a sign of poverty, of poor education; for the lonely, the homeless.

It was strange at first, and wonderful, when I came to realise that when I went the extra mile to help people in need, they stopped seeing that I wore a hijab, that I was a Muslim woman, and just saw me as a friend.

The garment worn by Mother Teresa and most orders of nuns is similar to the hijab. The Virgin Mary is usually portrayed with her head covered as a symbol of devotion and piety. Before the coming of Mohammed in the sixth century, Christian, Jewish and Hindu women showed reserve by covering their hair. Modern Western dress has swept this aside, but it remains in Muslim culture, not as a sign of difference for the sake of it, but of belief in a higher power; not as submission to man, but submission to God, to Allah. The woman on the bus wearing a headscarf is not challenging

British culture. She is just being herself. A tattoo may show allegiance to some group or party or interest, without challenging British culture. Likewise, a T-shirt with a logo or message. A headscarf says: 'I am a Muslim woman going quietly about my business and have no desire to offend anyone.'

Across Europe and in the United States, a woman in the hijab is often seen as challenging the status quo, making a silent attack on Western values. She is not. I dress to please myself. This is perfectly normal. Some women choose short skirts, décolleté dresses, scarlet lipstick and high heels that shape the body because they feel it enhances the way they look, because they are avid followers of fashion (whether or not it suits them), or simply because they like that attire and it makes them feel good about themselves.

Young Muslim girls have the same genetic drives, thus the continual battle between the generations and the hijab being just as controversial an item among Muslims as it seems to be to everyone else. For this reason, in 2013, the Bangladeshi American Nazma Khan launched in New York what has since become World Hijab Day. Celebrated annually on 1 February, it is a day to showcase a woman's right to freedom of expression and an invitation to other women to try wearing the hijab just for one day.

During the time of British and French colonisation, women were encouraged to remove the veil and emulate European women. As a consequence, in north Africa, Egypt and the Middle East, the veil and scarf became an emblem of national identity and resistance. Some women wear the hijab to simply show pride in their ethnic identity. There is no strict rule. There are first-generation Muslim immigrants in the UK who never wear veils of any kind, and their third-generation granddaughters wear a burqa. The greatest tragedy is for those who are never able to have a choice, so we make the choice because it is ours to make.

PART TWO

BEHIND THE VEIL

CHAPTER 4

OUR MOTHERS' GENERATION

Life for our mothers' generation was vastly different to that of today's cohort of Muslim women. When they first came to this country, not only were they in unfamiliar territory, but most did not speak any English, so they had few people with whom they could communicate.

When my father first came to England as a young man, he worked on the docks of the East End, which has a history of colonialism. The Lascars, seamen from the Indian subcontinent, south-east Asia and the Arab world, began to arrive in the UK in the sixteenth century, filling the gap in the labour market on merchant ships returning from India. Recruited by the British East India Company, the lascars were experts in seamanship, shipbuilding and port activities, and most of the City of London was built on the transatlantic slave trade. They were given less food and were only paid 5 per cent of white sailors' wages, despite being expected to work longer hours. They also played a significant role in Britain's military conflicts, including the First World War.

However, the first generation of women who came to the UK from the Indian subcontinent after the Second World War did so for different reasons – either to escape civil war, to join family members already here, or to accompany husbands seeking better employment opportunities. Many Pakistanis found employment in the textile industry in places such as Manchester, Bradford and other cities in Yorkshire and Lancashire. Others worked in car and engineering factories in Birmingham and the West Midlands, and light industrial sites in Slough and Luton. The biggest wave of Bangladeshi women arriving in the UK was in the early 1970s, when they fled civil unrest in their country and settled mostly in east London boroughs. Many of their husbands found employment in Indian restaurants following the collapse of the steel and textile industries.

The most important language my mother had to learn was not English; it was integration, and she did so with quiet dignity, even when racists called her a 'fucking wog' and a 'coloured bitch' as she pushed the pram down the street, with my sister and little brother in tow, or when a cashier would look down her nose at her and speak loudly as if she were deaf, repeating things when it was perfectly clear that Amma understood.

English people often seemed to see a foreigner's lack of English as a mixture of stupidity and a personal assault on the language they loved – even though they didn't necessarily speak it all that well themselves. Further harassment came from the fact that she wore a sari, had jet black hair that was shiny as a raven's wing, wore kohl on her eyes and lines of chiming bangles that ran up and down her wrists. She learned quickly to smile even when she was being insulted.

Our mothers' roles were generally centred around the family and home, whereas Muslim women today are choosing alternative life options, entering higher education and earning prominent positions in the workplace. Generational changes in education, employment and aspirations have helped to dispel stereotypes of Muslim women and open up greater opportunities. Despite this, people in the public eye are still making faux pas and using terms that are now regarded as politically incorrect, or even offensive.

In 2019, then Conservative Cabinet minister Amber Rudd referred to Britain's first black female MP Diane Abbott as a 'coloured' woman during a BBC radio interview. Although Ms Rudd's intentions had been good – the interview was given on International Women's Day and drew attention to the abuse faced by many female MPs, particularly those from ethnic minority backgrounds – her offensive and outdated use of the word 'coloured' indicated her grave lack of understanding of the experiences of black women and women from ethnic minorities. Her ill-thought-out words caused painful memories to resurface, including of my mother being referred to as a 'coloured bitch'. If a well-educated politician in her fifties is still using outdated terminology, what message does this convey to the rest of society?

Some people will wonder why saying 'a coloured woman' is so different from saying 'a woman of colour'. But 'coloured' is not just a word like any other. It is regarded as an offensive racial slur as it is intimately bound up with the history of racial segregation and inequality in the US, echoing the days when black people were ordered by the police department to wait in separate rooms, when they were forced to eat in different restaurants, sit in different areas on public transport and use separate toilets. Through its long history of being used to mark out people with darker skin, identifying them as different and 'inferior' to white people, the term 'coloured' carries layers of meaning that resonate painfully today, just as 'Negro' does. (Likewise, 'half-caste' and 'mixed race' imply that there is a pure race and that those who are not white are somehow impure. The advice now is to use 'mixed parentage' or 'dual heritage'.) For those who have never had these words hurled in their faces, the resonances may be more difficult to hear, but they ring out loud and clear to others.

In the early days of living in Kent, where there were very few families of colour, our greatest challenge was 'coloured integration', as my parents would term it in their own way. It was the everyday struggle of my father being referred to as 'the coloured worker', and my mother being called 'the coloured woman' by other parents and teachers at the school gates. We had a supermarket near our house and Mum used to take us with her to stock up on bread and other essentials. She would go in quietly and hush my brother not to make too much noise, while my sister sat patiently in her pushchair. I would watch as she nervously collected things from the shelves while young white male shop assistants made snide remarks beneath their breath. They would cast an annoyed glance in her direction if she dropped an item or could not find something. It was as though these impressionable young men were finding reasons to back up their beliefs and despise people of colour. Perhaps their views had been shaped by their parents, television or other areas of influence. They were only looking for fault, so naturally they would find it. They did not view white customers with the same disdain if they dropped something, or had difficulty locating a particular item.

Although I was young, I remember feeling distinctly uncomfortable and fearful that something bad was going to happen. What if they falsely accused my mother of stealing, or hurt one of us? I was afraid that my brother might start whining, or touching things, and I could not wait to leave.

On one occasion, my mother could not find eggs, so she waited for the shelf to be refilled. The assistant made us wait for thirty minutes and every time my mother asked how long it would take in her broken English, the young man rolled his eyes and snapped, 'I'll get to it in a bit; be patient!' His female manager heard him shout at my mother and asked what the matter was. The assistant replied, 'That coloured woman and her kids can't wait for their eggs.' I remember the large blonde woman with her red false nails screaming back, 'They can fucking well wait; what is it with fucking coloureds taking over in the shops?' She then screeched with laughter. All the other customers looked at us, and an elderly white woman rolled her eyes in disgust, as though we had the plague.

As we stood in the checkout queue, my mother was elbowed out of line. The cashier looked down her nose at her and spoke loudly as if she were deaf, repeating things when it was perfectly clear that she understood. I recall the times when I saw supermarket assistants remove goods from my mother's trolley, or replace other things with pork sausages, claiming that she might not be able to afford them. This was never done subtly, but in front of other customers, which was demeaning. Cashiers often tried to short-change her, assuming that because English was not her first language, she would not notice or would be too embarrassed to challenge it. So often it was done by white women of all ages. I never understood why they felt the need to keep humiliating a woman in front of her children and an audience of customers who were obsessed with what we had in our shopping basket.

On that day when we were waiting for the eggs, I remember feeling utterly humiliated. I was about eight years old at the time, but that feeling of humiliation stayed with me and is something I will never forget. Although people are no longer allowed to treat customers like that, I am fully aware that some people still hold those same outdated views of those who aren't white or have a foreign accent. I remember an elderly white woman pushing her way into the queue and my mother saying 'sorry', thinking she was in the way. Another white woman then decided that she was next and pushed in too. The manager allowed this to happen, as though we were invisible. That image of my brother peeking from under my mother's sari, my little sister sitting patiently in the pushchair and my mother trying to pay for her items in the right way is something that stayed with me for months to come. My mother smiled timidly at the assistant and the other customers, even though they scowled back; people with white privilege who justified pushing my mother because she was brown.

When we finally left the supermarket, I felt shaky, weepy and furious, but did not wish to upset my mother further, so I fought back my tears. However, my rage got the better of me and as we turned the corner, I took one of the eggs out of the bag without Mum noticing and ran back saying I had forgotten something. I went back into the supermarket and threw the egg on the till, saying, 'You gave us too much change,' before racing out of the store while wiping away tears of anger.

As I ran out of the shop, I heard the assistant scream, 'You fucking little Paki; it's the coloured woman's fucking kid… dirty monkeys coming over here.' When I reached my mother, she asked me why I had gone back. She was upset because of what happened, but became angry when I returned. I mumbled unintelligible words and she asked me again.

I was afraid to tell my mum what I had done, as I knew

she would be angry with me. To her, it was a white man's country and she didn't want us to get into trouble. So, I lied and told her I had dropped a marble (I was into collecting and playing marbles, which were all the rage at the time). She interrogated me all the way home as it was clear she did not believe me.

My memory of the incident did not go away and neither did my mother's suspicions. A week later, I went with Dad and one of my little sisters, a toddler at the time, to collect some groceries for breakfast from the supermarket. I dreaded every step I took and Dad eventually asked me if I was constipated, as I seemed to twist and turn in my stride.

When we got to the supermarket, there she was; the red-faced cashier. I could see that she recognised me. I was scared, and my heart raced, but the woman said nothing and just smiled at my dad, which I found a bit odd. She was very nice to him and struck up a conversation – a little too long for my liking – but threw daggers at me as I peeked from behind him. The more she spoke to Dad, the angrier I became. I stepped out and stood beside him, but she ignored me. As she scanned the goods, she asked him, 'Do you want to pop over to the George?'

My dad scratched his head and smiled back in confusion.

'You know, the pub, luv; do you wanna go down for a pint with me?'

I snatched my dad's hand.

'No, he doesn't!' I bellowed.

'I wasn't asking you!' she snapped.

My calm, collected dad, oblivious to the woman's flirtatious behaviour, shook his head and said, 'I don't drink. I'm Muslim.'

'And we're coloured, remember!' I added, vehemently.

This prompted the woman to tell my dad what I had done, while smirking at me.

'Shut up!' I screamed at her. But it was I who shut up when my father looked at me angrily and held up his finger for silence. The white woman sniggered at me. I started crying.

Tight-lipped, Dad collected the shopping, ignoring the woman and the white customers watching us. He took my hand and turned to leave, but before we did he said, 'My wife will never come here again. No more coloureds will come to this shop.'

From that day onward, we stopped shopping at the bigger supermarket where it was cheaper and instead began shopping at what used to be called Jordans, run by an Indian family. My dad made it his mission to encourage all his friends to shop at Jordans and we became close friends of the owners.

My brutal awareness of my mother's long, quiet struggle to be accepted for who she was explains why I reacted so strongly to hearing Amber Rudd's use of the derogatory term 'coloured woman'. Rudd's comments are reminiscent of my mother's experiences of facing the word 'coloured' every day. Its use perpetuates the normalisation of racism, which is still too often faced by women of colour in the UK – even fifty years after my mother's experience. I know that certain words and phrases are often uttered with no malicious intent; they are used simply in ignorance, or because they used to be acceptable terms. Even today, many people have said that they find it hard to keep up with political correctness, so can be forgiven for using a term that was once not considered to be insulting. Some people go further and argue that if they don't mean to be racist, it simply doesn't matter which words they use. The problem is that good intentions don't erase the pain caused by racial slurs, even ones spoken unthinkingly. White people are not experts in racism and cannot tell a person of colour that what she has experienced is not racist. If you say the same thing to two people and one is offended but the other isn't, does the person who wasn't offended have the right to tell the other that they are being paranoid, or that they don't have the right to feel that way?

All experience is subjective, so the best we can do is embrace each other's differences and listen to each other's perspectives, ensuring that all those who wish to be included are given that opportunity without question. People should not be judged on their race, but equally their identity should not be invalidated either. On the negative side, some might argue that being 'colour blind' is counterproductive, as it ignores discrimination and practices that disadvantage racial minorities, such as lack of access to the same job opportunities as white candidates. 'Tolerance' is often held up as a high ideal, with many applauding Britain for being 'a tolerant society' towards immigrants. But tolerating something means you don't really accept it but rather simply put up with it. What if we aimed higher than tolerance, for respect and inclusion?

My mother rarely replied to insults heard on the streets. She would say it is part of human nature; that the English see us as different, we are different, and that they will treat us as though we don't belong. She would shrug her shoulders in a resigned manner.

Although I prefer to focus on the happy memories at primary school, it wasn't always rosy. The unkind teasing was generally directed at me from a minority of boys and although it made me angry, I told myself that these prejudices had probably been learned – either from their parents or other sources. It was an example of how impressionable young minds are and how children tend to believe what they are taught. My mother loved plaiting my hair in a long, thick braid with colourful ribbons, completely unaware of the taunts I faced at school of 'greasy black poles' and 'Ribena ribbon'. It was lonely and painful being made to feel different, conscious that I did not belong to their 'group'. There were moments when I didn't want Mum to collect me from school because the mockery would increase for both of us. The need to mask aspects of my family's life in numerous circumstances led to frustration at the constant sacrifice required to adapt my identity.

In the first year of secondary school, I didn't want to walk with my mum through the shopping centre when she was wearing her sari or speaking in Bengali audibly, because of the constant stares, which were hardly inconspicuous. Maybe people assumed that we could not see them.

On Fridays, when it was Jummah prayers, it was all about cutting one's nails, applying 'Surma' – a kind of kohl that should never have been used as it contained lead – to our eyes and, of course, dousing ourselves in musk perfume from Saudi Arabia, sent to us by my uncles who lived there. Mum used to send me to school like this on Fridays when the other children teased me and called me 'Batman'. I think the boys secretly liked the look and kept coming near me to take in the soft fragrance of musk!

On the occasions that I wore a shalwar kameez for an event, I would avoid meeting school mates in the streets as I didn't want to face questioning, or possibly even taunts from the boys who called me names. Despite this reluctance, I felt more comfortable about my ethnicity when a white mother once said to me at school that I was 'different to other Pakis'. Although others might have deemed her words to be offensive, I understood the sentiment behind them; it was this woman's intention to make me feel welcome, and I did. I chose to ignore her use of the word 'Paki', whereas others listening might have cringed at a word that is now regarded as racist. I ignored it because I really didn't want to draw attention to it. It was my childlike way of dealing with the situation I found myself in. I don't think there was racist intent behind her words, as I sensed that she tried to put herself in my shoes and imagine what it felt like to be an outsider. It was about adapting and reconciling my values with what I understood of the struggles she faced in trying to accept me into her community using the limited tools at her disposal.

• • •

My mother, Amma, chose to stay and make her home in Britain. She settled her children in school and wanted to integrate in her own way – and one way was learning to cook traditional English food. Amma's forays into Western cuisine covered everything from Victoria sponge cakes to roasts. Her first attempt at a Victoria sponge was to make the cake in its entirety, including the butter icing and jam fillings in the mixture before putting it in the oven. Once she'd got to grips with the recipe, she began to throw in a few Bengali ingredients like ghor (date syrup) to give it texture.

I still remember when our neighbour came round to teach her the secrets of a great Sunday roast, showing her how to season and stuff the chicken and how to roast the potatoes. All the while, Mum held her homemade mixed curry powder in her hand, hoping to sprinkle a little on the bird.

Our neighbour put her hands on her hips saying, 'No, Lalita, we aren't going to currify the bird!'

Mum giggled back and said, 'OK, OK, just flavour a bit.'

'You can add an extra sprinkle of black pepper.'

When Mum was in charge, our Sunday roast chicken came with red chilli, cardamom and a pinch of saffron. Absolutely delicious, first generation Anglo-Bengali.

Then came fish fingers, chips, baked beans and salad. Every time, we still had to eat some curry and rice afterwards because, in her mind, it was the only food that could fill us up. I'm astounded that my siblings and I didn't end up obese.

My mother is British, just as she is Bangladeshi and Muslim. In all honesty, I think she would struggle to make her home in Bangladesh if she ever moved back. She raised five children in Rochester at a time when there were very few Bangladeshi women living near her. There was no one to whom she could relate. She was essentially alone in completely unfamiliar territory, with little knowledge on how things were done here, so it must have been terrifying for her. There were no support networks and she had to adjust to new social norms on her own. No matter how long you have lived in another country, you never lose your roots and values. My mum is a pensioner now, but we children still roll our eyes when she stares at other people who behave differently from what she is accustomed to. She doesn't understand the attraction of voyeuristic reality TV shows, or young girls wearing heels so high that they risk breaking their ankles. She was horrified when she discovered one of her grandchildren had made a TikTok of her watching her favourite Indian soaps.

My mother now has fourteen grandchildren, all born in Britain, whom she loves and shares a connection with in different and unique ways.

She combs their hair, encourages them to oil their skin until they glow, attempts to advise on fashion wear, tells them that grammar schools are the best, cooks 'Bengalish' dishes and loves her Eid and Christmas get-togethers.

What's not British about all of that?

CHAPTER 5

YOUNG, BRITISH AND HIJABI

In a 2016 speech, Prime Minister David Cameron said that 190,000 Muslim women in the UK spoke little or no English and that he planned to invest £20 million to enable them to do so. He said that a minority of Muslim men were 'perpetuating backward attitudes', feared the success of women, and inhibited their education and advancement. He may have had good intentions, but his speech indicated that he saw it as the 'white man's burden' to free Muslim women from oppression and give them more opportunities with the gift of the English language. Not only did his comments undermine the successes and positive achievements Muslim women were making; they fed into damaging stereotypes, stigmatising Muslim women as a group.

When the *Telegraph* reported that Cameron had privately suggested that one of the main reasons some Muslims were vulnerable to radicalisation was the 'traditional submissiveness' of Muslim women, tens of thousands of Muslim women of all ages used the hashtag #TraditionallySubmissive to tweet their professional and educational achievements. They also condemned Mr Cameron for 'throwing around lazy stereotypes', as one tweet suggested. One woman, Safina, tweeted: 'I am intelligent, articulate, opinionated, capable, adaptable and I can even make a decent soufflé. What I am NOT is #TraditionallySubmissive.' Another held up the following sign: 'Qualified Montessori teacher; fluent in five languages (including English); avid reader of books (in English).'

This uprising speaks for itself; talented, feisty and assertive Muslim women daring to challenge a white male politician on his blinkered views.

Paradoxically, the Prime Minister's comments encouraged evidence that a modern generation of British Muslim women were educated, confident and challenging traditional images of Muslim womanhood.

Nevertheless, we have to remember that there are differences between older generations of British Muslim women and those of today, although the same could be said of different generations of white British women and other cultures.

The original Bangladeshi migrants' children and grandchildren who were born and educated in the UK have entirely different experiences and expectations to those of their forefathers. They have not had to adapt to a new social, cultural and linguistic environment, even though many will continue to practise customs linked to their religion, such as having an arranged marriage. When the first generation of migrants arrived in the UK, unable to speak the language, it was natural for them to form communities with other Bangladeshis so as not to feel isolated. It is a similar story with other immigrants to the East End, such as the Eastern European Jews who moved into Spitalfields in the late nineteenth century to escape persecution, and the Somalis who were recruited to fight during the First World War. There was another influx of Somalis in the latter part of the twentieth century, who joined the already established community in London to escape civil war in their country.

The current generation of Muslims inevitably had fathers and grandfathers who worked on the docks or in the restaurant trade, while the women stayed at home and raised their children without ever questioning their roles. While traditional practice was that married couples would live in the household of the husband's parents and that younger wives would operate under the authority of their mothers-in-law, this no longer holds true for many in Britain. Multi-family households are still in the minority. In 2019, the Office for National Statistics showed that overall there were only 297,000 households containing multiple families (1.1 per cent of all household types), but this included all families, not just Muslim households.

Today, Muslim women expect more from their lives, with many ambitious young women achieving academic success and pursuing rewarding careers, while effectively balancing this with faith and family. Despite the challenges they face in the workplace as a result of Islamophobia and the false belief that they are voiceless, submissive and passive, more Muslim women than ever are in leading positions in society. In 2016, research showed that Muslim girls are more motivated to gain qualifications in order to survive in the job market and, for the first time, were outperforming their male counterparts. It also revealed that 25 per cent of Muslim women aged between twenty-one and twenty-four had degrees, compared with 22 per cent of Muslim men of the same age.

Despite pre-judgement and discrimination, an increasing number of Muslim women are breaking through these barriers to reach the top of their chosen careers. In May 2020, for example, hijab-wearing Raffia Arshad, aged forty, who is a successful barrister, was appointed a deputy district judge on the Midlands circuit. She said that she now wanted to make sure that the sound of diversity is heard loud and clear. Khadijah Mellah made history in 2019 when she became the UK's first hijab-wearing jockey and Jawahir Roble is the UK's first female Muslim referee, having achieved the English Football Association's Level Six qualification.

What some people don't realise is that education and the securing of academic achievements – for both men and women – is highly valued among south Asian families in Britain. This is backed up by a report from Liverpool John Moores University, 'Muslim Women and Higher Education: Identities, Experiences and Prospects', in which the empirical data gathered demonstrated how many Muslim women cited their families as key sources of encouragement and motivation towards higher education study and in thinking about future careers. Nevertheless, the report showed how the respondents' experiences of university were varied. One young Muslim student said that she chose her university because of its reputation for 'having a large and vibrant student Islamic Society' organising and holding events. The diversity among her course mates made it easier to integrate and be accepted. Another respondent studying Accounting and Finance said that because the Muslims on her course were primarily male, you couldn't tell that they were Muslim, whereas she wore the hijab, which made people think they had to behave differently towards her.

In what might come as a surprise to non-Muslims, Islam's modest dress code also applies to men. Some Muslim men will often wear a taqiyah (skullcap) during daily prayers and some will wear full traditional Muslim dress. Again, as with women choosing to wear the hijab, what men wear is purely down to personal choice. In addition, one cannot pigeonhole all Muslims in the UK as they are from different cultures, countries and Islamic theologies. Some may wear the traditional dress of their culture whereas others won't. Therefore, like most men of all cultures, wearing trousers and a long-sleeved shirt will not identify your religion, unlike a hijab that clearly identifies a woman as Muslim.

One might ask that if the hijab is enough to identify a woman as Muslim, why do some Muslim women still wear full traditional dress? Again, this is not a requirement but a choice. My mother, for example, wore a sari, kohl on her eyes and a line of bangles on her wrists. It was traditional dress in Bangladesh, and it was what she felt comfortable wearing when she first came to this country. One could ask the same question of women in any culture, religious or not. We've even seen white British women adopting cultural dress in certain situations, including Samantha Cameron, Elizabeth Hurley, Helen Mirren, Katie Derham and Theresa May. It was suggested disparagingly in a *Guardian* article that Mrs Cameron was 'resorting to copycat style to "fit in"' when she visited the Shri Swaminarayan Mandir, the Hindu temple in north-west London. Therefore, if a woman chooses to wear traditional dress here, why should she modify her style to 'fit in'?

A while back, a white male colleague said to me: 'I have never seen you in anything other than the traditional style of dress. Never jeans, never a T-shirt. Why does a modern woman such as yourself – who is a role model to so many young Muslim women – always have to wear leggings?'

Why should he need to see me in jeans? After all, not all white British women wear jeans or T-shirts, yet no one questions this. Some women prefer dresses and wouldn't be caught dead in jeans; others live in yoga pants and hoodies. What is this version of traditional style that he assigns to me?

As it happens, I do actually wear jeans when I'm walking in woodlands with my family, enjoying a break from city life, but I choose to wear something different in my professional life.

He went on to say to me, 'I think it is because Muslim women are required by the Quran to dress modestly.' Yet jeans can be regarded as modest dress when teamed with other items, so his argument there fell flat.

But the fact remains that I've never asked him why he always wears black suits, pale shirts and patterned ties.

It is all credit to Muslim women who wear the hijab with pride, knowing that it may attract unwanted attention, pre-judgement and even hostility. It is this courage and pride that sets them apart. These women are liberated by their veils, rather than oppressed. This is, however, not just a Muslim issue. Even in Christianity, women were guided by the Bible to cover their heads as a way of showing their dedication to God and their husbands. Chapel veils signified humility and modesty and were part of the early Christian tradition. In Orthodox Judaism, the practice of modest dressing and behaviour is known as tzniut and applies to both men and women. Many Jewish women also wear wigs, known as sheitels, or headscarves, known as tichels. Sikh men and women view the dastar (a type of turban) as a symbol of faith, honour, self-respect, courage and spirituality.

In 2017, the European Court of Justice ruled that employers were allowed to stop their staff from wearing religious headdresses, as well as other religious clothes and symbols – anything from a Christian crucifix to a Hindu bindi. During a debate on *Good Morning Britain*, Sahar Al-Faifi, a molecular geneticist, said that rather than indicating submission to some patriarchal model of modesty, for her the niqab was an act of worship, an act of devotion to God. She said that her mum and sister didn't wear it, and she found it a little patronising that someone who didn't share her faith should tell her what she should or shouldn't wear. She also said that she was completely against Muslim families ordering their women what to wear. Piers Morgan quite rightly pointed out that men can choose to wear thick, woolly beards through choice that conceal part of their faces without anyone questioning it. Since the Covid-19 pandemic reached the UK in March 2020 and the wearing of face masks in certain public areas became mandatory, attitudes towards women wearing face veils have changed dramatically. Muslim women have said that they are no longer seen as 'outcasts' or a 'security threat'. One woman said, 'Now I'm no longer a ninja and I'm no longer a letter box. Everyone is getting used to the face covering and no one seems to stare at anyone.'

It seems rather hypocritical that Western society appears more accepting of youths concealing their heads and faces beneath hoodies, people sporting a multitude of indelible tattoos and women wearing revealing clothing as a result of a male-dominated culture. Those who believe that a Muslim woman wears a hijab because of a man's directive fail to realise that she could be doing so for any number of reasons, in the same way that someone wearing revealing clothes might have various motivations to do so. If you asked most young women why they wear provocative clothing, some will say it was their choice, others that their choice was influenced by a man, or the desire to impress, or the result of peer pressure.

Is it harsh reality that these so-called cosmopolitan

societies are not really tolerant of others' beliefs and cultures? What about some elderly non-Muslim women who like to wear headscarves when they leave the house? Would governments consider banning those too?

Children of other religions also observe their faith through different elements of their appearance. One of the most distinguishing features of being a Sikh is not cutting the hair on one's head, while some Jewish boys have long, curly sidelocks (payots), and Hindu girls wear a variety of clothing such as shalwar kameez for informal events and tikas on the forehead for decorative purposes.

In November 2017, chief Ofsted inspector Amanda Spielman recommended that school inspectors should question Muslim primary schoolgirls about their reasons for wearing the hijab. She suggested that expecting pupils to wear the headscarf 'could be interpreted as sexualisation of young girls' – when the truth is that young girls are far more likely to be sexualised by the media and reality TV shows.

The debate on this issue only intensified when St Stephen's School in London, which had previously banned girls under eight from wearing a headscarf, tried to extend the rules to pupils under the age of eleven. It also pushed to impose an outright ban on fasting during Ramadan. The principal claimed the rules encouraged integration into modern British society. The Department for Education said that 'pupils' uniform is up to schools' discretion'. Naturally, this attracted backlash from many, including human rights activist Heena Khaled, who noted that the premise of the campaign to ban the headscarf on young girls was to protect them from being sexualised, but that 'there was no definition as to what sexualisation means in this context'. As she pointed out, young girls make the choice themselves rather than doing it because it is something that their parents have enforced: 'Some of them wear it one day and not the next.' She also asked when we were going to start talking about young Sikh boys wearing turbans, or young Jewish boys wearing the kippah. If this ban has been reserved for young Muslim girls, she said, then this is not only anti-Muslim but inverted misogyny, and such discrimination will only marginalise them further.

In her last year of primary school, my eldest child, Zakia, decided that she would take one of my favourite scarves and wear the hijab to school. She wore it every day with her friends. I recall one day when we were running late for school and she still wanted to put her scarf on, even though I was shouting at her to leave it. When she went to secondary school, Zakia began to take it off. She presented a bit of a challenge for some of her teachers, often saying what was on her mind, whether it was a good idea or not. On one occasion, she told one of her teachers who had applied for a senior position, 'You'd make a good deputy head, but not at our school.' Detention was duly served.

Some of Zakia's secondary school peers wore scarves, as did some of her new friends when she went on to university, while others did not. Some changed their minds between school and university. Zakia was proudly Muslim in everything she did, praying five times a day, trying to find a place for Muslims to pray at university, never breaking her fast, and reciting the Quran and her knowledge of Islamic history. It comes across in her everyday interactions, from etiquettes of good behaviour derived from Islamic teachings and alms-giving, to humility and saying sorry when she is wrong.

My younger daughter, Nabila, never wore a scarf at either primary or secondary school but over the past few years she has decided that she will wear the hijab, much to the delight of my mother.

Nabila chose to wear it, and Zakia admired her for it and encouraged her.

Over the years of wearing her hijab, Nabila has become more strong-willed and determined to make her own choices, regardless of what anyone else thinks she should do. She has become far more independent and has the courage to stand up for herself and others. From the little girl who couldn't stop talking to the shyness of her secondary school days when she struggled with illness, her hijab story has given her a sense of empowerment and strength to be who she is: unafraid and undeterred. Her choice of scarves, designing modest wear for herself as well as her friends and family (including me), has developed into an eye for design and fashion.

During the pandemic, when Nabila returned to work at a fashion retail store, she wore her uniform and hijab and settled back to a sense of normality at work after a long period of shielding. One Saturday, when the store was a little busier and a white male customer asked for her help, she obliged and directed him to the right aisle. He then sought help from her colleague – another hijab-wearing young Muslim woman – who also helped him.

The man returned to Nabila and said, 'Was it you that I spoke to just now? There's two of you with the – you know – thing,' gesticulating with his arms to demonstrate a veil around his head. Nabila replied, 'There are two of us, but we are different,' to which he responded, 'Oh, I hadn't noticed. You know, with the head thing, you all look the same.'

Tight-lipped, Nabila called her manager and asked her colleague to come to where she was and then said to the man, 'Now take a look.'

The pallid skin on his neck began to develop a crimson tint, which crept into his sallow face. The two young women were clearly different in physical appearance. Nabila was much taller than her petite colleague, with her skin soft tones of brown, deep slanted eyes, long lashes and high cheekbones, whereas her colleague from Yemen was much paler, with classical, fragile features.

Two beautiful girls in hijabs, not just different in appearance but in their life experiences, their likes and dislikes, who they may marry and what they want to do in the future. This would be the equivalent of saying that two men wearing black suits looked the same, even though they were of different heights and skin tones.

Their manager turned to the customer and sharply said, 'Maybe take a closer look next time – respect our staff.'

From my life experiences and watching my daughters grow, my belief is that whatever our ages, our ethnicities, class differences and status in life, when one part of our identity is under attack, demonised and assigned blame, we intrinsically feel the need to defend ourselves. That attack is personal and hurtful, so like all human beings we reach out to defend what is part of us. For Muslim girls and women, whether or not we wear the hijab, that choice becomes part of our identity, and it is natural for a woman to defend that identity when she is attacked or misrepresented. It is similar to a fair-haired woman (natural or otherwise) feeling that she needs to prove to someone that she is not a 'dumb blonde' after someone has assigned her that label. Stereotypes and generalisations ignore differences between individuals and therefore promote prejudiced attitudes.

It is to my daughter's credit that she challenged this man and hopefully taught him a lesson in the importance of looking at everyone as individuals and noticing the clear differences in physical appearance, regardless of how they are dressed.

Many people are probably still unaware as to why Muslim women wear a hijab in Western society. Most of the time, it is a personal choice. For some it might be a political, cultural or fashion statement, while others might just want to look like their mums and feel more grown up. However, it is not – as some may think – imposed on them by a parent or a man. A Muslim woman exercises freedom of choice in her attire in the same way as a white British woman, or a woman from any other culture. No one would consider asking a white British woman why she wears a headscarf, or a hat, or a headband – or even a crucifix.

Sadly, disparities exist within different interpretations of Islamic theology. The belief held by many is that Muslim women are oppressed, controlled by their husbands or families, and are expected only to raise children, keep house and attend to their husbands' needs. The truth is that the basis of Islam is equality for all humanity, regardless of race, ethnicity, class or gender. The younger generation of British Muslim women are questioning traditional images of Muslim womanhood. They are serious about their educational and professional goals and are performing exceptionally well educationally. They are determined to break out of the traditional mould to enter the workforce and promote a more cohesive society, showing that it is possible to become women of power and influence while still following one's faith. In doing so, they have become ambassadors of Islam, dispelling stereotypical representations of oppression and isolation.

The stereotypes associated with Muslim women do not all originate from religious beliefs. Some stem from misunderstandings of Islam; others have a grain of truth but apply only to a small minority. On many occasions, for example, I have been asked what number wife I am, with those asking

the question assuming that all Muslim marriages are polyga-
mous. Many think that Muslim women are prohibited from
participating in activities outside the home. Another myth
is that the Quran justifies violence against women, when
in fact Islam condemns all forms of violence and abuse,
and domestic violence is explicitly forbidden. It is crucial,
therefore, to debunk myths about Islam in Britain and to acknowledge that Muslim women in Britain are not a homogenous body; they are a diverse group with wide differences
in class, gender, political affiliations and religious beliefs.

As a second-generation Bangladeshi Muslim woman, and
the eldest from my family, I was aware of the difficulties I
might face in continuing my studies after secondary school.
Initially, I wanted to further my education and felt determined to battle against any discrimination. Maybe I felt
that I had something to prove to those who pigeon-holed
hijab-wearing women. I wanted to do more in life than get
married and raise a family and, in fact, I wanted to be a great
role model for my future children and show them that anything is possible with the right attitude. My mother was not
keen for me to go to university, yet she wanted me to have a
degree, which didn't make any sense. When I decided that
I would get married instead and pursue higher education
at university later, she still wanted me to obtain a degree,
perhaps feeling a bit more secure in the knowledge that I
was married and had additional support from my husband.
Her reluctance might have stemmed from her and my father's fear of the difficulties I might face at university, given

the discrimination that we had faced over the years. While this might have stemmed from cultural insecurity, ten years later there was a stark difference when my youngest sister pursued higher education at university and lived away from home. I think my mother realised that times had changed and that the future of her children was in building a life that would be very different to her own; that we expected more in terms of pursuing a career, raising a family and reconciling both of these with our continuing faith.

This highlights the changing behaviour of Muslim families in terms of confidence; from discouraging daughters from continuing with higher education to urging them on. There is no doubt that the new generation of Muslim women acknowledge that these restrictions on female education are deeply rooted culturally, in contrast to the Islamic principles on knowledge and education. Nevertheless, the deep-rooted history of discrimination towards women of all backgrounds has placed women in unfavourable positions in Muslim and non-Muslim communities around the world.

British Muslim women have challenged this traditional image through their participation in the education sector. More British Muslim women from Pakistani and Bangladeshi backgrounds participate in non-compulsory further education than their male counterparts. Dr Nabil Khattab of the Doha Institute for Graduate Studies in Qatar and Professor Tariq Modood of the University of Bristol suggested that one possible reason might be the fact that Muslim women appreciated that they were 'likely to face labour market penalties due to widespread stereotypes and racism, perhaps more so than Muslim men'.

Ever since the tragedy of 9/11, the media has propagated the idea that Islam is a violent and backward religion and culture. Unfortunately, those who have suffered most have been visibly Muslim women. Stereotyping has marked out veiled Muslim women as ideal targets when they are seen in public.

Myths about Islam and about Muslim women are deeply rooted in society: they are depicted in the collective consciousness either as heroines, defying their 'cruel' fathers and families in order to fit into Western society and benefit from all that it offers, or as victims, succumbing to their oppressive traditional culture. Unfortunately, stories like that of Shamima Begum have perpetuated the oppressed-terrorist-bride rhetoric, when these women form a tiny minority and are no more representative of British Muslims than Christian extremists are of the average Church of England believer. In the book *It's Not About the Burqa*, by Mariam Khan, Muslim women talk about their lives under the threat of a disapproving community and racist country, revealing the huge diversity of experiences and calling for an end to 'the lazy stereotyping, the misogyny and the Islamophobia'.

Muslim women are fast becoming narrators of their own story and have become independent and empowered to play an active and rewarding role in society.

Three decades after arriving in the UK, and now living in Tower Hamlets in a large Bangladeshi Muslim community,

I can see the difference in the aspirations of young Bangla-deshi and Muslim women – not just in Tower Hamlets, but across London and Britain as a whole.

I remember a family I supported, and their daughter Rima. Rima's mother came to live in Tower Hamlets when she was seventeen years old and could not speak English. Her husband's spoken English was better, but his written English was limited. Rima was the fourth in a family of five children: three daughters and two sons. While she was strong in maths, Rima was weaker in English – and although her parents invested in a tutor for her older brother, they would not do the same for her. They had an expectation that she would do her A-levels and work in a school, or for the council. Her older two sisters got married at eighteen after finishing their CSEs and went on to work as classroom assis-tants in local primary schools near their homes.

Rima wanted something more; she wanted to be a char-tered accountant. She had watched her father struggle over the accounts for his two Indian takeaway businesses, while her mother supported her dad and her older siblings to enable the business to function smoothly. Rima did her bit and because she loved numbers, she put her father's outgo-ing and ingoing invoices into a ledger to help him when he met with his accountant. Like other young Muslim women growing up, Rima could see the difference in standards of behaviour between Asian men and women, which she argued about with her parents. When she did her A-levels, choosing Maths, Economics and Sociology, it was all fine because she was in a girls' school. Had she attended a mixed school, then choosing subjects that were male-dominated might have been more of an issue.

'The biggest problem are the gossipers around here. Say I go to university and bump into a male friend and we get talking and someone from my estate sees me, the word will be "Rima's got a boyfriend,"' she moaned to me.

The year was 1995 and I had just had my first daughter. I laughed to myself and noted how things were still about 'keeping up appearances'.

Rima told her teachers of her dream to be an accountant. Instead of glowing with encouragement, they told her that it would be hard for 'an Asian girl in a scarf'. Though she was faced by these barriers, including those put in place by her parents, Rima was a determined young girl, and now and then I suppose I gave her an encouraging little nudge. Eventually, her father relented, and Rima was accepted to university.

However, Rima's troubles didn't stop when she went to university.

They are so old, the lecturers – old, so white and all men! And they keep going on about how being an accountant is usually a man's job. I'm like, so what? That's why I'm here. I didn't have a fight with my dad to get to uni and be told by some white man that I can't do the job.

It only got worse when one of her groups had a female lecturer for a while.

> What is it with white people? I thought that a female lecturer would understand. All she went on about is that the City might not give everyone placements, looking at me all the time. She then repeated, 'I'm just letting you all know', looking at me again and not at the others because they didn't wear a scarf.

It could be that the female lecturer was simply preparing Rima for the discrimination that she would face in the workplace. It reminded me of the way my mother tried to prepare me for not going to university, yet wanted me to have a degree. Human beings have strange ways of of trying to help each other; sometimes these result in misunderstanding. In addition to misguided advice from her lecturers, Rima also had to deal with jealousy from other young women.

> I go to uni because I need a degree, not a man. It's a bit hard telling the guys I don't want anything more than to work with them. Then the claws come out from the other girls, who believe that I'm competing with them. I really don't want these guys; they're welcome to them.

Rima needed encouragement, not a heap of negative vibes. There were work placements that seemed to go to favourites, or recommendations from lecturers, but being resourceful,

Rima managed her own placement and went on to work for KPMG years later. She persevered through a series of 'no's and 'perhaps next time's until she was offered a place.

There has been a slow but perceptible change in the attitude of today's Muslim parents towards their daughters' education. As older children have moved through the educational system and transitioned into work, it has become easier for younger siblings to persuade their parents to give them the freedom to choose their own career paths.

Most studies to date have concentrated on first-generation Asian parents, rather than second-generation British-born parents, so are the latter more accommodating of Western values rather than upholding traditional values? In a Gender and Education Study conducted by the Centre for the Study of Ethnicity and Culture and Birmingham University, which interviewed parents from several generations, the overwhelming response to the question of the importance of educating Muslim women was positive. All parents recognised the need for young Muslim women to achieve higher education. They did not differentiate between young men and young women, stressing that Islam does not discriminate on the basis of gender.

Albert Einstein once said, 'All religions ... are branches of the same tree. All these aspirations are directed towards ennobling man's life, lifting it from the sphere of mere physical existence and leading the individual towards freedom.' Though we strive for the same goal, the paths we take might be very different, and each religion is always open to different and shifting interpretations. Even within the same religion, what is right for one generation or family will not be right for another.

Younger generations of Muslims, who are often more educated and aware of the exact teachings of the Quran, feel that older generations lack comprehension of these teachings and are actually more likely to be bound by culture.

In a new generation of Muslim young women, I find that parents are corrected by their daughters. When parents are questioned about their beliefs on Islam, and then corrected by their children, they argue back and claim that what the younger people are saying will not be accepted within the Muslim community, even though their children are right. This causes conflict between them; a clash between culture and religion.

There are many dimensions, with some following their own understanding and influences, while others are locked in more orthodox environments. The older generation, for example, are more likely to be influenced by interpretations preached by community leaders or other powerful figures and place great importance on being respected and accepted within their community. This has sometimes caused alienation for young Muslim women who feel ostracised from the majority, and even their own families, because of their refusal to be 'schooled' into their ways.

I remember a young Italian boy who lived on our street. We used to walk home together from primary school with other friends. One day, my dad said that some people in our community might get the wrong idea of me. He said it ever so lightly. He told me that he understood, but that it wasn't acceptable in our community, so I whispered back, 'There's only us and we are the community.'

I didn't have relatives living near me growing up and I know that relatives can put a lot of pressure on families, whether they are Muslim or not.

There are parents who are happy to allow their daughters to choose their husbands, but then they succumb to pressure from other family members. I had no relatives here to place any pressure upon me or my parents, so I was quite lucky, although it could feel lonely at times.

Young Muslim women are successfully reconciling their faith, family and community commitments with education, work and a social life, even though many have struggled to fit in. It's all about balance and having to move backwards and forwards from different lifestyles and belief systems, especially if they come from an enclave that resembles the country from which their parents came rather than what is generally thought of as 'Britain'.

I have heard many young women say how difficult it is to make their parents understand that university life is different to the lifestyle they know, especially when their parents expect them to fit back into that lifestyle and way of thinking once they come home. They question the futility of educating themselves if they are unable to make their own decisions. However, eventually most parents and families understand – and are accepting of – their daughters' dreams and aspirations.

It appears that self-motivation and a desire to succeed and prove others wrong have been overriding factors in Muslim women pursuing their chosen careers. Some young women have talked about the challenges they faced when studying male-dominated topics at university, generally taught by white, middle-class tutors. However, the stereotyping and discrimination they have faced has made them even more determined to prove the doubters wrong and to be an inspiration to other young Muslims with similar aspirations. These hurdles never go away, but we learn to negotiate them. I see the struggles my daughters have encountered, as I did at the same age, and I see the ongoing challenges faced by the women I've supported through my work. The UK is full of courageous, creative and determined young women who are shattering stereotypes, challenging negative images and breaking down barriers, not by being controversial, but simply by being themselves – setting a positive example for young women of all faiths and nationalities.

CHAPTER 6

THE VEIL – A FASHION ICON

Muslim women don't just wear the hijab; they have built a whole fashion around it. In Islam, there are no set rules on the style of an individual's hijab, as long as it conforms to the simple guidelines of being loose, modest and non-transparent. Muslim women define their own styles while adhering to codes of modesty and elegance.

This chapter explores the concept of the veil in different Muslim communities and how Muslim women characterise and interpret modesty. The veil and hijab are more complex than we really know. They have become a statement of Muslim women's contemporary fashion sense, style and strength. How much of the wearing of the veil is with explicit reference to their faith and how much an adoption of changing ideas of style?

Our perception of our faith and the ways we choose to express it are inevitably coloured by our own life experiences and the norms we have grown up with. A Muslim woman's choice of clothing is not just influenced by her religion, but by her culture. In Indonesia, for example, it is commonplace for a Muslim woman to wear a simple veil teamed with a pair of jeans and a tight, long-sleeved T-shirt, or a loose tunic with a long skirt. In Malaysia, the favoured traditional dress is a knee-length, long-sleeved blouse or tunic and a long skirt, which is pleated on one side. The sari has a place in Hindu traditions as well, but for me it speaks to my Bangladeshi roots. A Chinese Muslim woman's experience of Islam will be different to that of an Eritrean Muslim woman. Similarly, the way we dress will be influenced by our cultural norms.

Some people may ask: how can a piece of cloth be both a symbol of oppression and a freely chosen accessory? The answer is that for the majority of Muslim women in the UK, the hijab has little to do with oppression; it is simply a matter of choice and a way of honouring one's faith, in the same way that some Christians wear crucifixes, Christian clergy members wear clerical clothing, and Hindu women traditionally wear saris. From my perspective, and that of other hijab-wearing friends, it is a personal choice – one that we have made freely and which has absolutely nothing to do with parental wishes or those of a spouse.

How does wearing the headscarf on the basis of modesty square with this passion for fashion, and that very human instinct to feel good in oneself? When I wear a scarf, it is about feeling good and connecting with myself and my faith in God. I do not need to sacrifice style or looking smart, elegant and attractive in order to follow my faith.

Many women feel empowered when they wear the hijab; it is not that they have any desire to broadcast their faith to others, but that they are saying, 'This is me; this is my style; this is my choice; this is about my personal relationship with God.' It has become a statement of independence, rather than patriarchal coercion as some falsely believe. Many women wear it to maintain a positive self-image and to be recognised as both British and Muslim. Hijabs come in a diverse range of colours, materials and styles, which can be coordinated with the rest of a woman's outfit without the need to compromise one's modesty. They can be combined with modern, fashionable clothes and are often incorporated into fashion-related images and advertisements. They have inspired new styles and been adopted by high-end designers and fashion houses. In 2016, Dolce & Gabbana launched a collection of hijabs and abayas and in 2017 Nike released its Pro Women's Hijab. In the same year, London played host to the first London Modest Fashion Week, held in order to shake off the clichés surrounding modest fashion. DKNY, Oscar de la Renta, Tommy Hilfiger and Mango have also designed one-off collections around Ramadan.

My younger daughter Nabila works in the retail fashion industry and wears the hijab with the store's uniform. She loves putting modest outfits together for all occasions, combining maxi dresses with trainers, jeans with oversized

jumpers, and long vintage skirts with high-collared tops –
all topped with her assortment of scarves of different colours and designs, and snapped on social media with friends
and colleagues.

Nabila is an example of how it is possible to wear modest
clothing in a Western context without compromising on
style. In recent years, the world of fashion has opened up,
enabling young Muslim women to blend Islamic values with
pop culture. Who said that Muslim girls don't have fun?

Throughout my life I have found that just as global fashion changes, so does Muslim women's fashion, with trends
coming and going with the seasons. Muslim fashion com-
prises a blend of culture and style and shows how traditional
fashion can be modified without compromising modesty
– and the two influence each other. In fact, so popular is
modest clothing becoming that women of all cultures are
choosing outfits that are less revealing from mainstream
stores such as Topshop, H&M, Mango, Zara and Gap. If you
visit any fashion store, you will inevitably notice a generous choice of wrist-length sleeves, high-necked dresses and
tops, wide-legged trousers and longer hemlines – aimed not
solely at Muslim women but at everyone. In addition to the
high street stores offering modest clothing, many high-end
brands including DKNY, Dolce & Gabbana and Tommy
Hilfiger have designed similar ranges.

Diane Pernet, American-born international fashion blogger and critic and founder of the ASVOFF international

fashion film festival, is known for her iconic black veil, which she wears despite being non-Muslim. She has expressed her individuality through her veil and dark glasses, which have become her trademark. In her 2018 interview with *Mind Mag*, entitled 'Beyond the Veil', Diane said, 'It's not a matter of trends or fashion. It's about making clothes that are timeless, that you like to wear until they fall apart. Fashion is about quality, personal vision, textiles, and colour. Even though I wear black. I think fashion, and what I look for, is desire.'

The interviewer also commented:

By the end of our conversation, I understood how misleading the austere uniform that has come to define Diane can be. The unrelenting black and completely covered person initially appears aloof and unapproachable – the definition of closed off … In a strange turn of events, I came to realize this fashion icon, quite literally, wears her heart and values on her sleeve, or veil as the case may be.

Diane's appearance has been celebrated rather than criticised – so why are Muslim women who have expressed both their personal style and their faith by wearing the veil constantly criticised and under scrutiny? As demonstrated by the interviewer's initial perception of Diane Pernet, a veiled Muslim woman may convey the impression that she does not wish to engage with anyone. Some may view this choice of attire not as an expression of personal style but as a requirement imposed upon them by a controlling husband or family.

Throughout history, women around the world have been subject to both societal conventions and formal regulations that dictate what they should and shouldn't wear. In the 1890s, for example, it was considered proper for women in the UK to cover their whole bodies in public, so necklines stopped just below the chin and hemlines always extended to below the ankles. In 1942, the US introduced Regulation L85, which dictated that skirt lengths should be no longer or shorter than seventeen inches above the floor. Although the move was prompted by wartime rationing, no rules were introduced for men's clothes.

One of the benefits of living in the UK today is having the freedom to wear what we want. Although we may still be guided by social conventions and fashion trends, women as a whole are freer than we ever have been to exercise our personal preferences and express our individuality through our choice of attire.

For Muslim women, though, that freedom comes with particular scrutiny. Those who indulge stereotypes still claim that Muslim women's hijabs (and, by extension, their faith) prevent them from engaging in public life, which is untrue. In some Western democracies, a Muslim woman's personal choice to dress as she wishes is still being denied, with a ban on the burqa enforced in countries including France, Belgium and Denmark.

This, of course, is rather ironic considering the 2020

coronavirus pandemic has made the wearing of face masks mandatory in many public places. Satvinder Juss, a London-based lawyer and human rights expert, said that legally, women wearing the burqa in Europe are now on much 'firmer ground' as result of the health guidance around face coverings. He went on to say that if, for example, a French police officer were to challenge a woman for wearing a burqa or niqab in public when everyone around her was wearing a face mask, the officer would 'clearly be engaging in religious discrimination and sex discrimination', which is forbidden under the European Convention on Human Rights.

For decades, fashion brands have catered for the maternity market by producing modest, loose clothing, and even swimwear has been designed for those who prefer to cover up. However, the burkini – modest swimwear for Muslim women – sparked another controversial debate. Despite the fact that revealing string bikinis are accepted on beaches across the country, France was once again at the forefront of discriminatory legislation, banning the burkini in several towns on the basis that wearing such a visible symbol of one's faith was in contradiction to France's secular values. In 2016, French police confronted a woman on a beach in Nice, forcing her to remove some of her clothing. Another woman also said that she had been fined on a beach in Cannes because she was wearing leggings and a headscarf. A witness said that people were shouting, 'Go home' and applauding the police.

Similarly, in some US states, Muslim women have been

persecuted for wearing a modest bathing suit and told to leave pools and beaches. A Huffington Post article in 2019 described the experience of one young Muslim woman, Manar Hussein, as she decided to venture to the beach for the first time in years – and for the first time since starting to wear a hijab in her teens. Her long absence from the water was due to the lasting memory of an experience at her local swimming pool in New Jersey, when pool-goers harassed a burkini-wearing woman, claiming that her swimwear was unhygienic. Nevertheless, wearing black leggings and a bright pink swim tunic with a black hijab, Hussein courageously ignored other swimmers as she ventured into the water.

Whether it is the burkini or the bikini, regulating what women wear can be a political act. In the late '50s in Italy, for example, the wearing of bikinis was prohibited because they were regarded as too revealing and immodest. Fast-forward to today, and women are being told to dial down their modesty. Throughout history, national legislation, local regulation and social pressure have dictated how women should dress, much more so than for men – and these rules have most often been determined by men. In the 1980s, for example, some American corporations had extensive dress codes for women. Professor Deirdre Clemente of the University of Nevada said, 'There would be four pages on what a woman could wear to work, and four sentences for men … The implication is that women are unable to regulate their appearance themselves.'

While some progress has been made, the current trend towards turning modesty into a battleground harms all women, Muslim and non-Muslim alike. Many women, of all faiths and none, prefer to cover up in the sun to protect their skin, and others just don't feel comfortable showing off their bodies. In Australia, a sun protection campaign began in the 1980s with the slogan 'Slip! Slop! Slap!' This stood for 'slip on a shirt', 'slop on sunscreen' and 'slap on a hat', in an effort to combat soaring cases of skin cancer. In 2011, TV chef Nigella Lawson wore a burkini on an Australian beach because 'it is incredibly comfortable and you're not getting a tan'. Is this, therefore, a case of double standards? Are non-Muslim women ever criticised for wearing modest clothing or a headscarf? Rarely. One could argue that this suggests a Western fixation on Muslim women's bodies, or even anti-Muslim sentiments, because the only difference here is religion.

In the UK, the burkini is slowly becoming more widely accepted, sold not just by Muslim retailers but in high street chains such as Marks & Spencer and Sports Direct and online at Amazon and eBay. In 2019, Nike introduced the Nike Victory Full-Coverage Swimsuit, a two-layer tunic with an attached hood and matching trousers, to cater for Muslim and modest swimmers. Speedo also offer what they call 'modesty suits', their version of the burkini. By broadening their ranges and considering all women, these companies are filling a much-needed gap in the market and boosting the economy by attracting the significant spending power of Muslim consumers.

Of course, Islamic fashion in the West is nothing new. In the 1980s, ethnic grocery dealers in Europe and the US began importing fashion clothing aimed at the Muslim population, which has proved to be highly successful and lucrative. Capsters have been selling the original sports hijab since 2001, followed by other Muslim-owned companies, such as Asiya and Sukoon Active. When high street brands follow suit, as Nike did in 2017 when they introduced the Pro Hijab to cater for Muslim female athletes, they not only generate financial gains but help to build a future of inclusivity and acceptance.

Alarmingly, a 2017 Pew survey showed that 62 per cent of participants answered 'No' when asked if Americans see Islam as part of mainstream society, and 75 per cent said that there is a lot of discrimination against Muslims in the US. However, as the fashion and beauty industry is welcoming Muslim models and designers, the false idea of Muslims as outsiders is hopefully changing. Muslim women are frequently featured in fashion campaigns, beauty adverts and high-end magazines, and modest-fashion influencers have become popular on social media. Many brands have recognised the importance of becoming more diverse and the significance of equal representation.

Not all of these moves are universally popular, however: brands can find themselves in the vanguard of progressive change, with public opinion lagging some way behind. In 2019, French sports merchandise store Decathlon found itself in the midst of a social media backlash after its plans to market a runner's hijab in France sparked intense opposition. Apparently, 500 people had complained about the product being marketed and staff had even been insulted and threatened. Decathlon initially defended the move to 'offer ... an adapted sport product, without judgement', noting that it was a response to the needs of some runners, but backed down in the face of political furore. Aurore Bergé, spokesperson for Emmanuel Macron's La République En Marche party, called for a Decathlon boycott on Twitter and said, 'My choice as a woman and a citizen will be to no longer put my trust in a brand that breaks away from our values.' How ironic that France's motto, 'Liberty, Equality and Fraternity', does not extend to women wearing the hijab or a company whose aim is to promote inclusivity and make its products accessible to customers of all ages and backgrounds.

Over the years, I have seen a shift in the heated debate over the veil as Muslim women who wear it – and those who do not – have fought for its respect in Western culture. While France remains reluctant to allow women to exercise freedom of choice, it's clear that global perceptions are changing. For some, the veil is still a symbol of female oppression or the threat of Islamic fundamentalism, but for many, many more it represents womanhood, faith and fashion – and there is a growing acknowledgement that aggressive opposition to the veil erases the experiences and voices of those who choose to wear it.

The hijab has been represented in art for centuries and is

still inspiring many artists today. In 2016, the educator and actor Deepak Ramola was inspired by an interaction with a young Syrian woman in Hamburg who had been called a terrorist for wearing a hijab. Under the collective art statement #UndertheHijab, he invited artists to contribute illustrations to break down stereotypes around hijab-wearing women. Deepak said, 'I want the women who wear hijab to know that they should not give anyone the power to weigh their worth. As one of the artists, Poornima Sukumar says, "May the stigma disappear like smoke in thin air!"'

One such stereotype is that Muslim women have no interest in fashion or beauty, which is a huge misconception. According to the State of the Global Islamic Economy, the Muslim spend on apparel and footwear is predicted to be around £317 billion ($402 billion) by 2024. Not only that, but as a result of the pandemic, with more people working from home and fewer social engagements, it's likely that comfy, modest attire will become the norm for non-Muslims, too. By 2030, the Muslim middle class is expected to increase to 900 million globally, which will further drive consumption. In 2017, the first Muslim fashion show took place in the Saatchi Gallery, Chelsea, set up by modest-fashion company Haute Elan. The event organiser and founder of Haute Elan, Romanna Bint-Abubaker, said, 'The Muslim market is currently the fastest growing global consumer. One in three people – by 2030 – will be a Muslim in the world – that's a huge population.'

Many fashion and gift retailers have recognised the

financial benefits of catering to the Muslim community; it is not just luck that Muslim women can now shop in fashion stores that previously catered primarily for non-Muslim women but a result of a conscious effort to appeal to a broader audience. Muslim women's clothing has become a booming industry, proving that diversity pays dividends. As well as releasing modest-wear ranges, mainstream stores like Debenhams and Nike have begun to run promotions for Ramadan and Eid. Luxury retailers in London gear up for the 'Harrods Hajj', a pre-Ramadan influx of wealthy shoppers from the Gulf. Net-a-Porter has organised Ramadan promotions in recent years, while Argos, Amazon, Etsy, Not On The High Street, food hamper companies and countless others offer Eid gifts.

Muslims are not just part of mainstream society; they are huge contributors to it. A new generation of Muslim women fashion designers, stylists, beauty bloggers and makeup artists from around the world have emerged and are exerting their influence. Contemporary Muslim Fashions, organised by the Fine Arts Museums of San Francisco, was a major exhibition which ran between February and August 2020, exploring the rise in the modest-fashion industry and showing how Muslim women have become arbiters of style both within and beyond their communities. Seventy-five per cent of the designers, artists and influencers in the exhibition were Muslim women under forty years of age. In Britain, the Muslim fashion industry is becoming a huge market led by strong Muslim women, many of whom wear hijabs. One

influential blogger is Amena Khan, who runs her own fashion company, Pearl Daisy, and was the first woman in a hijab
to be featured advertising shampoo. In one of her Instagram
posts she said, 'Woman dressed in a mini skirt = provocative. Woman wearing a hijab = provocative. The message
here? Dress how YOU want to dress – their being provoked
is their own problem ... Nobody deserves to feel unworthy
or belittled for who they are.'

In June 2020, Amena decided to stop wearing the hijab,
purely through personal choice. She said:

> I wore the hijab for as long as I did because it was my
> choice and I never felt oppressed by it. I never felt that I
> was not being myself, I fully embraced it ... you should
> strive in your life to be and to pursue what your heart
> wants and don't let anyone ever tell you otherwise because
> my hijab did not hold me back ... nobody forced me to
> wear it and nobody forced me to take it off.

The beauty of technology and social media is that Muslim
women now have a wider platform on which to showcase
the many different ways of understanding and practising
Islam while still being forerunners of style and fashion.
Muslim women are defining their own styles, showing that
modesty and beauty are completely compatible and that it
is possible to create an outfit from regular, high street chain
stores that conforms to their desire to follow their faith.

They have the same appreciation of perfume, makeup and accessories as non-Muslim women and put a great deal of effort into looking attractive.

In 2019, Nurul Shamsul was the first veiled woman in New Zealand to participate in the Miss Universe New Zealand beauty pageant contest. She said that Muslim women need to be modest and should not be chasing validation or approval from others for their looks. However, she said that it was important for her to enter the contest in order to pave the way for girls and show that it is possible to be beautiful, fashionable and modest at the same time.

Her comment about not chasing validation or approval from others could be likened to arguments against second-wave feminism in the late 1960s and '70s when its supporters tried to encourage women to discard anything that men might use to objectify them; in this case, makeup. Some women argued that a socially appropriate appearance that included makeup was important for the workplace and other situations. To those arguing in favour of discarding cosmetics, the fact that these women saw makeup as essential in order to be taken seriously in society just proved the effectiveness of the patriarchy. This will always be a divisive issue, as many women – myself included – wear makeup to please themselves, not men or anyone else. It's simple: I enjoy wearing it. However, there are women who wear it to appear attractive to others, and to feel accepted, but that in itself is probably a sign of insecurity.

The first time my niece showed me a Barbie doll she wanted, I thought it was going to be the traditional blonde, fair-skinned Barbie. In fact, what she wanted was a Muslim Barbie, complete with a hijab, whose outfit had been designed by Haneefah Adam, a 26-year-old medical scientist and artist based in Nigeria. Haneefah posts images of her dolls on Instagram so that young hijab-wearing Muslim girls can identify with them. She said that when choosing who to model a doll upon next, she looked for women who are positive examples for young Muslim girls. Some of the influential women she has based her dolls upon include Ibtihaj Muhammad, the first US Muslim Olympian to compete while wearing a hijab, Melanie Elturk, co-founder of online hijab store Haute Hijab, and Ilhan Omar, a former refugee, the first woman of colour elected to the US Congress to represent Minnesota and also the first Somali-American elected to Congress.

Through the power of social media, many Muslim women are succeeding in dispelling myths and becoming respected bloggers and fashion icons, inspiring a new generation of young Muslim women who are proud of their identity and not afraid to make their voices heard. In 2014, I was interviewed for a *Sunday Times* article about the rise of Muslim beauty blogs and how young British Muslim women are reconciling the wearing of the hijab with cosmetics. I said how encouraging it was to see young women growing increasingly confident in their identity over the past two decades.

These are women who want to be recognised by society for what they do as individuals. When asked how I viewed the apparent paradox of the Muslim beauty blogger, I said that Islam tells a woman to look after herself and be healthy. Therefore, if she wants to care for her hair and body, she's doing it for herself, not anyone else. That's an empowering sentiment to share with the world.

CHAPTER 7

HANDSHAKES, HYGIENE AND THE HOT HIJABI

One Christmas, my nephews and nieces had a sleepover as my son was approaching his first birthday. The living room was strewn with sleeping bags, pillows and blankets and, of course, the obligatory snacks. Sitting in front of the TV, the younger children happily munched on crisps while watching the four Pevensie children exploring the fantasy world of Narnia. In the scene where Lucy meets Mr Tumnus, she approaches him slowly as he hides behind a tree. She asks him why he is hiding from her and he replies that he didn't want to scare her. When Lucy introduces herself and offers Mr Tumnus her hand to shake, he looks confused, so she explains, 'You shake it.' When he replies 'Why?' Lucy says, 'I don't know. People do it when they meet each other.' The children burst into laughter.

In the Western world, the handshake is a standard and

acceptable way to greet someone, regardless of gender – or at least it was until the emergence of Covid-19. The handshake has been in existence for thousands of years, and although there have been different theories regarding its origin, most of these are related to trust and respect. Some have suggested that it was originally a way of conveying peaceful intentions, as the extended hand showed that the person was not carrying a weapon, and the up-and-down movement of the shake would dislodge any weapon that might be concealed in the sleeve.

For many Muslims, and particularly Muslim women, though, shaking hands is not a reflex gesture. For those who aren't already aware, some Muslim women don't shake hands with or hug anyone of the opposite sex. This is just part of the concept of modesty within the Muslim faith, which includes no physical touching between members of the opposite sex if they are not married or closely related. In the advent of the Covid-19 pandemic, touchless greetings have replaced handshakes as the norm, and the children were already highly attuned to this cultural difference.

Zakia said she had once seen her teacher pick his nose at a parents' evening and then shake hands with a parent. She had made sure that I didn't make the same mistake by pulling my hand away and lecturing me about not shaking hands because I was a Muslim woman – even though she had just given a high-five to the school police officer on her way in. The teacher had looked surprised, but Zakia could hardly tell me in front of him that it was because he had just had his finger up his nose.

'Urggghhh, yuck!' shrieked all the children together. They giggled and began relating their experiences of where people's hands could have been, wondering if the Prime Minister washed his hands or used hand sanitiser every time he shook someone's hand.

I would warn people in public life: please be careful where your hand has been before you hold it out to shake hands with someone; children are watching.

Regardless of religion or gender, everyone has the right to consent to how they are touched, and this includes actions that seem as innocent as holding or shaking hands. Greetings vary across cultures, so we should respect an individual's right to greet other people in a manner that is acceptable to them. Some Europeans give each other a kiss on both cheeks, whereas the Japanese bow to each other.

Some Muslim women don't mind shaking hands and some do, so until you know, it is respectful to wait for her to offer her hand to you first. I will freely hug female friends and acquaintances I am close to if they are also huggers, but not men. I know many non-Muslim women who feel uncomfortable hugging anyone, as it is an invasion of personal space, and others who don't like shaking hands because the hygiene aspect makes them feel uncomfortable. We can only assume that others wash their hands as often as we do and don't cough or sneeze into them. There are many ways of greeting someone without the need to shake hands or hug. One could argue that it's better not to shake hands at all than to engage in a handshake while feeling awkward, which the other party will inevitably pick up on. We often hear people joking about a weak, 'limp fish' handshake, a bone-crushing one, or the captive one where the person holds onto your hand for an uncomfortable period of time. The point here is that we should respect everyone's personal space, regardless of whether they are friends, family, co-workers, clients or strangers.

Some people have taken umbrage at Muslim women refusing to shake hands, however. In 2018, for example, a Muslim woman in Sweden was awarded financial compensation after she made a claim for discrimination when she refused to shake hands in a job interview. Farah Alhajeh was interviewed for an interpreter role at a language services company in Uppsala, north of Stockholm. She placed her hand on her heart as a polite greeting but was immediately shown to the lift. The court subsequently ordered the company to pay her £3,900 in compensation.

Also in 2018, a university academic in New Zealand was sacked for trying to shake a Muslim woman's hand, because he accused her of sexual discrimination when she refused. The University of Auckland terminated his employment on the grounds of 'serious misconduct', saying that the academic was fully aware that shaking hands with a Muslim woman was culturally and religiously inappropriate.

Two years earlier, in 2016, a Muslim woman left her job as a supply teacher in Helsingborg, Sweden, after she refused to shake hands with one of her male colleagues. Although the woman preferred to put her hand on her heart and bow as a greeting, the school principal said that the male colleague concerned felt 'tremendously discriminated against' and that she must conform to the school's 'core values'.

From a British legal perspective, the right to freedom of religion and belief is protected by the Human Rights Act 1998. Yet there are still those who feel offended by a Muslim woman exercising her beliefs. Living in multicultural Britain, we cannot operate from a one-size-fits-all perspective. Maybe these different customs and beliefs should be included in the school curriculum to avoid future embarrassing situations, rather than adopting the belief that if we don't belong to that culture then we shouldn't have to learn about it. This is something that my family and I experienced from a minority of other children and their parents when I was at primary school. I recall that my classmates didn't understand why I didn't eat meat dishes at school, as it was not halal, but did eat meat and poultry at home. They would talk about me as though I looked down at them. 'She doesn't eat sausages, Miss, because they're not good enough for her. They have their roast chicken at home – more for us at school!' It was only later, when I began talking more about faith through the celebration of Eid, that my classmates and teachers began to understand a little more. Embedding diversity and multiculturalism within the primary school curriculum will foster understanding and acceptance and make children less likely to develop false perceptions or prejudices.

In 2020, as I write this chapter, we live in a pandemic era where the handshake is on hold due to the risk of contracting and spreading coronavirus. Some people are even questioning whether we will shake hands ever again. Gregory Poland, an infectious disease expert at the Mayo Clinic research institution, called the handshake an 'outmoded custom', adding, 'When you extend your hand, you're extending a bioweapon.'

Before his own coronavirus diagnosis, Boris Johnson shook hands with everybody. On 3 March, the same day SAGE recommended the government should advise against shaking hands and hugging, the Prime Minister told a press conference, 'I am shaking hands continuously,' and he was photographed doing so over the following week. On 27 March, he announced that he had tested positive for coronavirus and on the afternoon of 6 April he was admitted to hospital. Because it is ingrained in British society, even Prince Charles kept forgetting not to shake hands, before offering a namaste gesture instead. He was also diagnosed with coronavirus in March 2020.

Just as it has with face coverings, coronavirus has made us reassess the way we greet each other, and how we approach many other aspects of our daily lives, both in work and in play. Although this change has been wrought by a particular set of circumstances, our current situation shows that our cultural norms are not immutable. Just because the handshake is an acceptable form of greeting in certain cultures, it does not mean it is disrespectful if someone does not reciprocate.

The word that everyone will inevitably associate with the Covid-19 pandemic is 'unprecedented'. It is a word that we are probably tired of hearing – from politicians, business owners, scientific advisers and many more; yet it is a word that sums up these extraordinary times and what may be the most difficult situation that we have had to face in Britain for more than seventy years. Hopefully, it has made more people appreciate the things that they have always taken for granted; even down to being able to nip into a supermarket without having to wear a mask, stand in a long, socially distanced queue or walk in a one-way system through the aisles. It has given us an understanding of mental well-being, of the difficulties faced by those who were living in isolation prior to the pandemic, and of the importance of keeping in touch with family and friends. People who were not previously au fait with the internet, Zoom or WhatsApp have learned new ways of communicating with their loved ones, and many companies have realised the benefits of homeworking.

We may see a decrease in rush-hour traffic and commuting, as more people continue to work from home, and we may look at how companies conduct business with each other, favouring remote communication over face-to-face meetings. In turn, this may reduce air travel, a move which will only benefit the environment in the long run. Hot-desking may become a thing of the past and work shifts may be staggered to avoid overcrowding in offices and factories.

It is certainly a situation that has revealed people's true colours; complainers, blamers and good Samaritans. The Covid pandemic brought out the best and the worst in us, from panic shopping, deliberate disobedience of social distancing rules and failure to wear face masks to altruistic people who have taken this as an opportunity to help other people, regardless of their own circumstances, and without any expectation of reward.

Although Covid-19 will never be as catastrophic as malaria, the bubonic plague or war, it is still a disease that can affect anyone, regardless of socio-economic status. However, amidst the gloom and doom, it has its bright side. The lockdown encouraged many people to take up new hobbies or rekindle ones from the past, such as art, baking and growing their own vegetables, and to realise how fulfilling and therapeutic this can be.

Changes have been made, therefore, that we can hope will be permanent, and perhaps finding alternatives to hand shaking will be one of them.

• • •

As we have now entered an era where we wash our hands more frequently and carry hand sanitiser with us, will our bathroom habits also change?

Growing up as a Muslim meant that using toilets out-side our house was a problem for me, as we use ablution to cleanse ourselves after we use the toilet. In Muslim house-holds, there will be an ablution jug and the sink will be close by if we need extra water to clean after using the toilet. Going to school and finding no ablution jug was a problem for me, but a bigger problem for my mum, for whom the concept was akin to having to use a bathroom with no sink available to wash your hands afterwards. I will never forget using the toilet in primary school for the first time and discovering that there was no jug or pipe to use to cleanse oneself. When I came home and told my mum, she looked at me in horror and marched me straight to the bathroom to have a bath.

Using an ablution jug is not just a Muslim practice but is also prevalent in other countries and cultures. In fact, the Western practice of wiping with tissue paper is viewed as less hygienic to many. In 2019, during his UK debut perfor-mance, Egyptian comedian Bassem Youssef joked, 'I don't get it: you guys are one of the most advanced countries in the world. But when it comes to the behind, you're behind.'

No one can deny that water cleans more effectively than paper and, of course, is less abrasive. Most people are familiar with the French bidet, which emits a jet of water for cleaning after using the toilet. The bidet is also popular in Italy, Portugal, Japan, Argentina, Venezuela, Uruguay and Paraguay. In China and Korea, they don't have toilet paper available, so you have to bring your own, and in Vietnam they use water cleansing. Flushable wet wipes have gained popularity in recent years, although the reality is that many of these are not truly flushable and therefore not eco-friendly, so with the current emphasis on protecting the environment, some people are opting for more expensive biodegradable wipes.

Toilet paper also contains formaldehyde and bleach, which can irritate the skin. If one were to accidentally get faeces on any other part of the body, it would be absurd to just clean it off with a piece of tissue paper; the natural response would be to clean it thoroughly with soap and water. Why should it be any different for one's behind? Research shows that people who use bidets suffer from fewer urinary tract infections. Although discussing toilet habits may seem a strange topic, they are an everyday function and we could learn a great deal from the bathroom etiquette of other cultures.

This topic has its amusing side too. Zul Othman, a project officer for the Australian government who has researched cultural and historical attitudes towards toilet facilities, said that he has witnessed the stubborn Western insistence on using some form of paper taken to its extremes. One of his Sheffield classmates ended up using a £20 note to wipe after the toilet paper ran out.

• • •

Every year when summer approaches, I brace myself for the same old question: 'Are you hot in that?' At a workplace summer event, my younger sister – dressed in a long, flow-ing dress with a scarf secured around her face – happily made conversation with her colleagues. The sun was beating down and my sister's colleagues were dressed in sleeveless tops and shorts. A white female colleague had been glancing at her continually while she chatted with other colleagues. Mehera was fully aware of the conversation that would ensue, as we Muslim women are attuned to certain looks which speak volumes.

The colleague concerned said to Mehera, 'It's lovely weather, isn't it?'

'Yeah, it's so nice – and better than the rain,' Mehera replied.

'It's a bit hot, isn't it?' the woman continued, looking Mehera up and down.

'Yes, it's warm.' My sister's irritation was beginning to show as she thought: 'Just ask the question.'

And then it came.

'Are you hot in your scarf?'

'No, I'm not.'

But it was the next statement that made Mehera angry.

'I suppose you've been conditioned to wear that cloth.'

Mehera was angry with her but contained her feelings. Did the fact that she had a job and earned her own salary not show her colleague that she was not 'conditioned' to do anything?

Calmly, she responded, 'I've only just started wearing the scarf more often. As for conditioning, well, you've been conditioned to wear your shorts and top in hot weather, but I think that's normal.'

The woman looked shocked and said defensively, 'No, I haven't been conditioned.'

'Yes, you have,' Mehera continued, determined to prove the hypocrisy of this woman's statement.

'No, I haven't.'

Mehera put her drink down and patiently explained that the woman had been brought up to accept that certain clothes were normal for her, so she needed to understand that Mehera had been brought up to accept that other clothes were normal for her.

We saw in Chapter 6 how throughout history, in all parts of the world, women in particular have been subjected to a raft of rules and regulations regarding what they can and can't wear – and they have often been penalised for breaking unspoken, unwritten 'rules'. In 1999, for example, a rapist walked free after the Italian Supreme Court claimed that the fact that the complainant had been wearing tight jeans meant that she couldn't have been raped; she must have helped the rapist remove her jeans, the judges ruled, because it would have been an impossible feat on his own. The ruling was eventually overturned, almost a decade later, but we have heard on many occasions how some rapists have used the way a woman was dressed to justify their heinous actions, with comments like 'She was asking for it, dressed like that'. Public opinion has gradually become more progressive, and today most would agree that however a woman chooses to dress, her clothes should not provide an excuse for those who would threaten her safety and her life. Until relatively recently, however, these excuses have been indulged – even endorsed – by many, however unthinkingly.

While 'conditioning' may seem a strong word, one's parents and the culture in which one is raised usually influence our choices. This is the point that Mehera was trying to make to her colleague.

Mehera ended the conversation and said to the woman, 'Now get yourself another cold drink; it will help you cool down.'

As the Muslim author Heba Alshareef has pointed out, 'We wouldn't think of asking someone wearing a miniskirt in winter, "Don't you feel cold?"' But the 'Hot Hijabi' question is so commonplace from non-Muslims, both men and women, that we anticipate it with amusement.

One hot day, at an afternoon open air event, a friend and I had worn saris with scarves. I remember how we both went through the best hijab fabrics for the summer, from linen, cotton and georgette, to rayon, silk and jersey. We decided that soft georgette would be a good choice. During the event, a pale (but not stale) male smiled at us repeatedly. My friend and I kept smiling back and then I began talking to someone. My friend, who is very curvaceous, kept smiling back at the man, and he returned the gesture. Under her breath she said to me, 'My lipstick is going to crack if I stretch my lips any further.'

When you know that someone is staring at you, it is

difficult to avert your gaze and curiosity tempts you into glancing back, even if it is unwanted attention. Particularly as a Muslim woman, you anticipate the awkward questions that people are itching to ask, or else you are seen as mysterious and a flirtatious challenge to non-Muslim men.

Eventually, my friend gave up reciprocating the smiles.

Pale Male decided to venture over and try to make small talk. These situations are so obvious to Muslim women, as we encounter them time and again. The small talk is just a poor prelude to the questions the other person is longing to ask. It amuses us, and it would be easy for us to embarrass them before they launch into the predicted questions, but it is far more fun to play the game.

'Hi,' said Pale Male. 'I just thought I'd ask if I could refill your glass with some more wine?'

My friend said, 'We're having cranberry juice.'

'Ah, it's hot; maybe some ice. You both look lovely.'

Her beautiful arched brows rose immediately, making her eyes look even larger, and I grinned, feeling sorry for the white man in front of me. I gave my friend a sideways glance, knowing what was coming next.

'You must be hot in the turban.'

We both smiled, trying our hardest to suppress a groan.

'It's not a turban; it's a hijab. And I'm even hotter without it.'

With her friendly response, my friend demonstrated one way of de-escalating a potentially unpleasant conversation. Whether we are faced by an ignorant comment such as this man's or a deliberate provocation, instead of responding in anger, one can begin by validating the other person's feelings, as most prejudices are learned and based on one-sided, limited information. We can view it as a conversation rather than an argument, and if we lower our voices and remain calm, the other person will be more likely to listen. By refusing to engage in heated confrontation, we might not always win the argument, but we can at least put across our points and agree to disagree. You never know what positive impact our words will have on someone, even if they don't admit it. Sometimes it's the way in which we respond that can win over people, especially in the case of Islamophobes abusing us, and white feminists forcing their ideology of liberation onto us.

It certainly doesn't help the situation when those in authority, who are supposed to be setting an example and denouncing prejudice, are actually perpetrating it themselves. In the UK, and Western society in general, we have what some people would term the 'Taliban Police' or the 'Halal MI5', those in authority who keep an eye on Muslims' every move; viewing us all with suspicion, even those working for their organisations. In 2011, for example, *The Guardian* reported how Muslims inside the FBI describe a culture of fear and suspicion. The article stated: 'Muslim FBI officials are alarmed that their religion and national origin is sufficient for the bureau's security division to treat them as a counterintelligence risk, a career-damaging obstacle that their native-born white FBI colleagues do not encounter.'

In the UK, the Prevent strategy was introduced in 2003 as part of the post-9/11 counter-terrorism approach. The idea was to prevent individuals being radicalised, but in my experience and that of many people with whom I interact, the general feeling is that this strategy has uncovered the practice of Islamophobia and excessive surveillance of Muslim communities taking place within government institutions. Data from ethnographic fieldwork suggested that institutional Islamophobia is embedded into policies and practices that routinely prioritise white interests over the interests of ethnic minority groups. Even as far back as the 1980s, a Chicago suburb was the target of the FBI's suspicion. Film director Assia Boundaoui made a documentary entitled 'The Feeling of Being Watched' after she suspected that her family's Arab American neighbourhood was still under FBI surveillance. Assia's suspicions were confirmed when she uncovered tens of thousands of pages from FBI documents that proved that her neighbourhood was indeed under blanket surveillance and the subject of one of the largest counter-terrorism investigations conducted in the US prior to 9/11. The investigation was code-named 'Operation Vulgar Betrayal'.

In 2013, *The Independent* ran a feature on five Muslim community workers who accused MI5 of waging a campaign of blackmail and harassment in order to recruit them as informants. The men were allegedly given the choice of working for MI5 or facing detention and harassment in the UK and overseas. Each of the men were told that if they did not help the security services, they would be regarded as terror suspects.

In the UK, many Muslim women feel that they are constantly viewed with suspicion, with many people assuming that they don't have voices of their own and are being controlled through fear by extremists. The media certainly has not helped to diminish fears of Islam, particularly since the 9/11 tragedy.

In order to help people reassess their views, to educate and to bring both Muslim and non-Muslim women together, in 2009 I organised an event entitled 'Behind the Hijab' to coincide with the release of an anthology of thought-provoking articles and poems of the same name, written by women from all backgrounds and cultures. The aim was to dispel the myths surrounding the hijab and to celebrate each other's creative achievements as part of International Women's Week.

Celebrities also have the power to influence people's views through their words and behaviour. We constantly see high-profile people inadvertently promoting racism through ill-thought-out comments on social media or public behaviour.

In the face of this suspicion and discrimination, some women have opted to remove their hijabs to conceal their Muslim faith; others have chosen to wear headscarves in defiance and to proudly display their identity. In 2014, Sumreen Farooq was abused on a London street, after which she decided to take a stand and wear a headscarf. In fact, the chairman of the Muslim Women's Network UK said that more women had chosen to wear headscarves following the 9/11 and 7/7 terror attacks. Whether women choose to wear the hijab in defiance, or remove it, both are an expression of individuality and demonstrate that what we wear is a personal choice, regardless of how others view us.

• • •

The media, books and movies have an enormous influence on people's views, even though much of the time they are presenting opinions rather than facts. What we read and what we watch shape our world, especially if we do not question what we are seeing. Nevertheless, occasionally a movie or series is released that presents controversial themes and includes multifaceted perspectives. Netflix drama *Elite*, for example, explores Islamophobia in Europe where three working-class students, one of whom is a hijab-wearing Muslim girl, upset the status quo. Another good example is *Enola Holmes*, a mystery film in which Sherlock Holmes's sister searches for her mother in London, but the main theme is the fight for women's rights.

I write this amidst the furore surrounding the action-based remake of Disney's *Mulan*, which has been hit by waves of criticism. The call for a boycott by Hong Kong's anti-government movement has come about following the film's leading star Liu Yifei's comments in 2019, when she posted #IAlsoSupportTheHongKongPolice with a heart emoji. It was also revealed that scenes from the motion picture were filmed in Xinjiang – the western region in China where the ruling powers are allegedly detaining, oppressing and 're-educating' millions of Uighur Muslims.

I am reminded of the Emperor's words to Mulan, as he and China bow to honour her in the climax of Walt Disney's 1998 animation. 'I've heard a great deal about you, Fa Mulan. You stole your father's armour, ran away from home, impersonated a soldier, deceived your commanding officer, dishonoured the Chinese army, destroyed my palace… and you have saved us all.'

Mulan's feisty character ignored tradition and law by disguising herself as a male soldier to serve in the Chinese army. The film showed a young woman of strength and independence, whose fate did not depend on a man. Her courage and bravery spoke volumes to girls and women across the globe – including my own daughters and nieces – telling them that they too could be the hero of their own stories.

Mulan's character is a departure from Disney's traditional depiction of heroines and princesses through her ethnicity, culture and heroism – the only daughter of an ageing army veteran who challenges gender stereotypes. Mulan is the story of a daring young woman who saves an empire, exploring compelling themes of family, honour, duty and the eternal tale of how good prevails over evil.

Disney had originally planned for Mulan to be to be an oppressed Chinese girl who was saved by a British prince with whom she elopes to the West. The movie was going to be an animated short entitled *China Doll*. However, director Tony Bancroft envisioned Mulan to be a different Disney heroine; strong, tenacious, and independent. Her words in the 1998 animation, 'I have to do something', resonate with many Muslim women.

Despite the many barriers we face – whether it's stereotypes around our ethnicity, our religion or the way we dress – we are successfully participating in diverse sectors of society, and serving as role models for future generations of Muslim girls. We are proving that we do not conform to other people's definitions of us; that we cannot be defined purely by our religion or the clothes we wear. We are as diverse as our white counterparts, both in our personal and professional lives, whether we are doctors, teachers, police officers, secretaries, politicians, accountants or homemakers. Muslim women are also uniquely placed to solve problems faced by those in the community who feel disengaged, or don't have the confidence to speak for themselves, particularly if there is a language barrier. Muslim women have the skills and understanding to help communities integrate and encourage their contribution to the UK's economic, cultural and civic life. Whether we shake a hand or not, look for an ablution jug or go without, whether we are hot or not in our hijabs, we can be women of courage, female empowerment and compassion.

PART THREE

UNDERCOVER – THE POLITICS OF THE VEIL

CHAPTER 8

ISLAM, INEQUALITY AND INTEGRATION

The debate around Islam, inequality and integration has changed with the passing of time. Britain now faces the threat of radicalisation and extremism, fuelled by ISIS. Unfortunately, social media plays a big part in recruiting young people as ISIS members can use it to encourage them to travel to Syria and Iraq by celebrating and promoting an image of success. They convince them that ISIS is the winning side and can offer them an exciting life. They portray their 'Caliphate' as a utopian state where Muslims will find status and belonging, and state that Muslims have a personal duty to support them. They twist Islamic terminology to suit their personal agenda. While thankfully rare, instances of radicalisation are often used to fuel distrust towards young Muslims in Britain and to reinforce the image of them as outsiders with suspicious intentions.

Against this backdrop, Muslim women in particular have

struggled to carve out their place in British society. How can Britain increase integration when Muslim women are still labelled 'submissive' and white men feel emboldened to tear their veils away from their hair?

We have to ask ourselves what the concept of the veil means, both for Muslim women and for those who question it. Is it simply beautiful attire and a personal choice to express one's identity, or is it a symbol of integration in a changing modern Britain?

Right-wing and nationalist forces have long exploited the veil as a symbol of separation or oppression, pointing to it as something to fear. When I worked on the Isle of Dogs during the time Derek Beackon was elected as a councillor for the British National Party, I remember Combat 18 running rampage on the island, and the Muslim grocer who faced a pig's head being flung through his shop floor at Castalia Square in broad daylight, whom I supported at this turbulent time. I remember assisting two Bangladeshi families – one prior to the election, and one after Beackon was elected – with an emergency transfer due to the hostility towards them. One mother had her headscarf pulled when she was taking her primary-aged children to school and the racists screamed 'Rights for Whites', the slogan used for a BNP campaign in the area. The local police had to send female officers to escort young children to their Quranic classes.

In the midst of these troubling and hate-fuelled times, I recall a white woman who began to harass her elderly Muslim neighbour for planting coriander alongside the flowers in her front garden on a council estate. The white woman had lodged a complaint against the Muslim woman because she had chosen to plant coriander and not English red roses. When I visited her as part of our community work, I remember her words: 'You'll find English roses in white people's front and back gardens, not some stupid herb. She's gotta learn to be like us – British.'

I asked the woman whether her neighbour had broken her tenancy agreement, broken the law, caused her noise-related nuisance, taken drugs, or smoked so heavily that the smoke wafted into her home. She answered 'No' to all of these questions and looked puzzled.

The complaint was not upheld.

One of the reasons there appears to be animosity towards a Muslim woman in a veil or niqab – and suspicion about the Muslim faith – is the minority of extremist views and distorted interpretations of religious texts. So often I have been told that my faith is a violent religion and that it seeks to kill, but this is not true, and millions of Muslims should not be judged on the false beliefs and actions of a tiny group of extremists.

On Tuesday 11 September 2001, as I cradled my daughter Nabila while she drank milk from her bottle, I was watching the television when the breaking news about the Twin Towers attack in New York was announced. Along with everyone else, I was totally shocked, deeply saddened and angered by this senseless act of terror. At the same time, I felt anxious, knowing that some people would assume that all Muslims harboured the same views as the terrorists. In my opinion, the extremists are not Muslims: they have just skewed the texts to fit their homicidal agenda.

Nevertheless, following 9/11 the debate regarding Muslims became polarised. I and many of my Muslim friends received sympathy from those who understood that we did not condone these barbaric actions and who were concerned about our wellbeing. On the other hand, there were those who assumed that this was an act of Islam and consequently showed animosity towards anyone who was visibly Muslim.

A University of Birmingham report on Islamophobia in the EU after 11 September 2001 found that Muslim communities and other vulnerable groups had become targets of increased hostility, and that a greater sense of fear among the general population had exacerbated existing prejudices and fuelled acts of aggression and harassment in many European member states. It further stated that Muslims, especially Muslim women, asylum seekers and others, including those who 'looked' like Muslims or Arabs, were occasionally targets for aggression. Mosques and Islamic cultural centres were also widely targeted in retaliatory acts. This will only get worse in Britain and Europe as we face the threat of radicalisation, the lingering menace of ISIS and the covert return of jihadi fighters from the fallen Caliphate in Iraq and Syria. According to the Counter-Terrorism Preparedness Network in its 2019 Anti-Radicalisation Report, the threat from terrorism has not diminished, but become more complex, with contributing factors including isolation and deprivation.

The annual survey by the anti-Muslim hate monitoring group Tell MAMA reported a 326 per cent rise in hate crimes in 2015, with many completely unprovoked attacks on Muslim women, including acid attacks and physical assault.

Then came the 2016 referendum campaign for Britain to leave the EU, during which Nigel Farage's UKIP displayed posters showing a lengthy queue of largely non-white migrants and refugees which sported the headline 'BREAK-ING POINT'. The underlying message was that migrants and refugees were a threat to Europe and that it would be a wise choice for British people to make sure the English Channel remained a secure barrier to keep them out.

Future Prime Minister Boris Johnson backed the Leave campaign, despite claiming that the decision to do so was 'agonisingly difficult'. Though of Turkish origin himself, Johnson warned that 77 million Muslim Turks could move to England if Turkey gained admission to the European Union – despite the fact that Turkey was (and remains) nowhere close to fulfilling the eligibility criteria and that any new members must be approved unanimously by existing member states, allowing the UK to veto Turkey's admission.

There were claims that many people voted Leave because they were stirred up by real or imagined fears about immigration. It's certainly true that in the weeks following the referendum, there was a significant increase in the number of hate crimes, particularly towards Muslim women wearing Islamic clothing. For girls in a headscarf, travelling on buses and the Underground became a daily game of dare. In November 2016, a report by *The Guardian* stated that in light of the Brexit vote, the prevailing concern within the Muslim population in Manningham, Bradford was that 'emboldened bigotry and Islamophobia' threatened to marginalise Muslim women to the point of exclusion. In December 2016, the Casey Review, conducted by Dame Louise Casey, reported that of the Islamophobic incidents recorded in 2015, 75 per cent of female victims were visibly Muslim as a result of wearing a hijab or niqab. The review also backed up assertions that the EU referendum had sparked increased reports of racist and xenophobic hatred.

In May 2018, Tendayi Achiume, the UN's special rapporteur on racism and xenophobia, said that hate crimes had risen starkly since the EU referendum and that anti-migrant and anti-foreigner rhetoric had become 'normalised' even among high-ranking civil servants. The United Nations Committee on the Elimination of Racial Discrimination added that 'British politicians helped fuel a steep rise in racist hate crimes during and after the EU referendum campaign'. Hate crimes reported to the police increased by 42 per cent in the weeks before and after the EU referendum. Even so, the police believe that only one in four incidents are reported to them, so the true numbers are likely to be much higher. Nor has the situation improved in the years since: in October 2017, 2018 and 2019, the Home Office reported successive annual increases in hate crimes recorded by the police, with the latest figures showing 47 per cent of religious hate crime offences targeted against Muslims. In London, Birmingham and Bradford, 'Punish a Muslim Day' letters were delivered in March 2018 urging people to carry out violent attacks against Muslims and offering rewards for acts ranging from verbal abuse to torture and bombing.

Amidst this climate of violence it is perhaps unsurprising that some Muslim communities, for instance in Bradford, have remained conservative and somewhat segregated, claiming that this helps them to feel safe. However, locality has a major influence: pockets of the Muslim community in Bradford are very dissimilar to those of London's Muslim community. As with all capital cities, life tends to be more progressive than in smaller cities and towns. In London, while there is still significant deprivation, the current generation of Muslims are achieving well educationally and frequently going on to pursue lucrative careers. Boroughs with a large Muslim community, such as Tower Hamlets, are nestled right next to the affluent City, which has an influence on the aspiration of young people. A census report conducted by the Muslim Council of Britain in 2015 showed that in a number of London boroughs, the population of Muslims in the 'higher managerial, administrative and professional occupations' category exceeds the number in the 'never worked and long-term unemployed' categories. In January 2021, Bradford was voted as being the fourth worst place to live in the country out of a list of fifty towns and cities, and it is one of the worst affected areas for rising unemployment. With a Muslim population of 24.7 per cent, there is still work to be done in Bradford to enable better integration and to address both ethnic and class-based segregation. Poverty and access to opportunity plays a part in this too.

When I travel through Stamford Hill and see the Orthodox Jewish community, it reminds me that all communities have their choice of how to live, just like I do. That is how it should be: no one should be persecuted because of their choices, as long as they do not hurt anyone else, and everyone should respect the fundamental rights and freedoms that are set out in the Human Rights Act 1998.

Feeling safe is crucial to all individuals and communities, in addition to cohesion and feeling that they are not viewed negatively, or under suspicion, especially in light of political rhetoric linking Islam to terror, and some newspapers' and politicians' negative portrayal of Muslim communities. In turn, revenge attacks, including those on mosques such as in Manchester in 2019, have heightened fear among Muslims and particularly women who are obviously Muslim.

For the past thirty years at least, amidst waves of suspicion and hatred towards Muslims, it has been hijab-wearing women who have faced the brunt of the harassment and intimidation. Certainly, in my experience and that of many other Muslim women I know, those of us who wear veils have experienced far more discrimination, verbal abuse, prejudice and even physical attacks because we can be clearly identified as Muslim. In the aftermath of past terrorist attacks, for example, Muslim women who wear the hijab have been targeted more often than usual. Islamophobia has impacted their job prospects and affected the way in which they are treated in the workplace.

In September 2019, *The Guardian* reported a 375 per cent rise in Islamophobic attacks on Muslim women in the week following Boris Johnson's infamous 2018 'letter boxes' comment. In the same month, I wrote an *Independent* article about this, venting my frustrations at the irony of how Mr Johnson on one hand opposes the banning of veils in public yet wrote that it was 'absolutely ridiculous that people should choose to go around looking like letter boxes'.

I questioned whether the debate had become more about the objectification of Muslim women than their identities, successes and aspirations. I have spoken to so many Muslim women in my ward who have told me how they have been left out of conversations in the workplace, at school and many other meeting scenarios, with some people believing that they don't have anything to contribute, let alone a voice of their own.

The weekend Mr Johnson made his 'letter box' comment, I went on a trip with a group of women, and a male passenger allowed us to board the train first. One of the women was wearing a niqab, and she was the last of us to get on the train. After spotting her, the man laughed and said, 'Hold on, you forgot the letter box.'

For the man it was a joke. He didn't think he was being unkind. He was simply quoting Boris Johnson. But in exercising his right to free speech he was being offensive to all of us. These kinds of stereotypes and labels, even used in jest, affect people's confidence and empowerment, and the flawed assumptions that lie beneath them only serve to fuel discrimination and ostracisation.

Nor is Boris the only world leader to fuel these prejudices. In 2016, President Donald Trump mocked the mother of a deceased Muslim war veteran when her husband delivered an emotional speech to the Democratic National Convention. Mr Trump said of Ghazala Khan, who stood next to her husband, 'If you look at his wife, she was standing there. She had nothing to say ... Maybe she wasn't allowed to have anything to say. You tell me.'

For years, Muslim women have been accused of not integrating into Western society, but the sad fact is that many of them have faced huge challenges in being accepted, even though they are keen to engage fully in civic life. The idea still seems to prevail, particularly in Europe, that Muslim women are oppressed and do not have the permission, aptitude or drive to pursue rewarding careers or engage in the same activities as non-Muslim women. If we are to make progress, we must challenge the stereotypes surrounding Muslim women, and dispel these myths of subjugation and a lack of professional ambition.

As a British Muslim woman working in a predominantly white, male arena, I have had my own experiences of prejudice and discrimination, which have often helped me to reflect on the wider political conversations occurring around the world. The topic of oppression has so often been brought up by white male acquaintances. I've even been asked what number wife I am, but the main question frequently asked about my veil (or hijab) is: 'Is the veil really a choice, or is it a symbol of oppression?' People have every right to ask and, as Muslim women, we should respond in a way that helps others understand the subject, rather than seeing questions as a challenge. Let us not fool ourselves: without doubt, there are women who live in family units where they are forced to wear the veil. But there are people of all colours, cultures and religions who have husbands, wives, parents and other family members who dictate what they should wear, what they should do and to whom they may speak. And just as women from distinct cultures and religions choose to dress in the clothes they want to wear and decorate themselves in ways that please them, with piercings, tattoos and extreme hairstyles and colours, so, beneath their veils, many Muslim women also have pink, green, purple or blue hair, teeter around at parties in dangerously high heels and contribute to the profits of the international cosmetics market. Controlling relationships are not just a Muslim issue, and the twin assumptions that a woman in a veil has had it foisted upon her but a woman in Western dress has considered nothing more than her own preferences are both equally flawed. So what is really going on when people interpret the veil as a symbol of oppression?

One hot day, when I was working for Tower Hamlets Council procuring placements for young people, a colleague concerned for my welfare said he wouldn't mind if I took off my headscarf in the heat. I told him that I would take off my headscarf if he took his trousers off. He laughed. I was joking, but there was a nuance to my comment I don't think he understood. His underlying feeling was that wearing a scarf in a council office was so abnormal that I must be wearing it against my will, and I needed to be given permission by him, as a man, to remove it.

Paradoxically, there is also the false belief that wearing the hijab, as a choice, constitutes deliberate non-conformity, or a challenge to the 'traditional' British way of life. This, in turn, leads to the misconception that a hijabi might not have the ability or willingness to perform or fulfil certain professional, parental or personal roles. There are undoubtedly companies, though few would admit it, who feel that employing hijab-wearing Muslim women would affect their brand or image.

But if the hijab symbolises oppression to some, then aren't most women oppressed, regardless of faith, by feeling that they need to look a certain way to earn the approval of others, particularly men? In 1972, on an entrance exam for a trainee programme at Merrill Lynch, one question asked was: 'When you meet a woman, what interests you most about her?' Astonishingly, the correct answer was 'beauty'. Low scores were given for those who answered 'intelligence'. There was, of course, no similar question relating to men.

We may have made great strides in gender equality since then, but it's easy to forget how recently some of those gains have been made. In the 1950s and '60s, the average married woman did not work outside the home but was expected to spend her time raising the children and keeping house. It was unusual for women to go to university, especially working-class women. Schools prepared girls for this life by giving them lessons in cookery, needlework and household management. (Essentially, the latter was a full-time job as they did not have all the electrical appliances that are available today.)

It wasn't until the 1970s that we saw the 'Quiet Revolution', with women enrolling in universities in much larger numbers, opting to work after marriage and entering professions that were previously regarded as male preserves, such as engineering. In 1975, the Sex Discrimination Act made it illegal to discriminate against women in employment, education and training, and in 1979, Margaret Thatcher became Britain's first female Prime Minister.

For Muslim women, the process of carving out their place in the workforce has often been fraught with added difficulties. Many south Asian Muslim women were engaged in informal economic activity in the 1970s and '80s prior to migration and first took up supplementary work in Britain in order to contribute to the household income. But with constraints such as language limitations, their options were more restricted; often they would work from home as machinists for the textile and clothing industry, a sector rife with exploitation and underpayment. During this era in Manchester, Pakistani Muslim women proactively created support networks, empowering them personally and professionally. In London's East End, many Bengali women worked at home machining, but by the early 1980s the Brick Lane clothing industry faced serious competition, particularly from Eastern Europe. Regardless of their level of education, this presented a problem for these women, as language capacity, discrimination and lack of confidence were key barriers to accessing alternative employment.

Nor have we made as much progress in overcoming these barriers as we might like to think. When I was first elected in 2010 I met many families, not just in my ward but across the borough, the city and the country, who spoke to me about the challenges they faced in many aspects of their lives because of prejudice and stereotyping. One Muslim woman, for example, was asked by a prospective employer if her husband minded her going out to work; others did not even reach the interview stage. Many Muslim women were inspired by my success and were also relieved to be able to talk to someone who understood their struggles; someone who would campaign for their voices to be heard. Many of the issues discussed were reflected in a report published in 2018 by the Institute for Public Policy Research (IPPR): 'Reaching Out: Tackling disengagement among Pakistani and Bangladeshi women in Britain'.

In spite of the fact that qualifications and educational attainment have improved significantly over the past twelve years, the report stated that a significant proportion of Pakistani and Bangladeshi women are still being let down by mainstream services, including on employment and mental health support. Although community-based support is critical in tackling disengagement among ethnic minorities, many community groups are locked out of funding and others are too small to access public sector contracts. In April 2011, the then Prime Minister, David Cameron, warned that immigrants unable to speak English or unwilling to integrate have created a 'kind of discomfort and disjointedness', disrupting communities across Britain. However, it was not about unwillingness, but the inability to afford English classes as, in the same year, David Cameron's government restricted the funding of classes in basic English to immigrants claiming jobseeker's allowance and employability skills allowance. Those claiming income support and other benefits were no longer able to attend classes for free. Disengagement is therefore most apparent in the labour market.

In December 2016, the Casey Review highlighted the link between English language skills and integration. It identified English language as 'a common denominator and a strong enabler of integration', with an impact both on social and economic integration. The report recommended prioritising improving English language skills as a way to reduce exclusion, inequality and segregation. Nevertheless, this is only possible if free English language lessons are made accessible.

In my borough of Tower Hamlets, ESOL (English for Speakers of Other Languages) funding was cut in 2009, with the loss of half of its ESOL courses. Overall, between 2009 to 2019, ESOL funding was cut by over 60 per cent.

The 2018 IPPR report also stated that while 71 per cent

of men from Pakistani and Bangladeshi communities are in employment, only 38 per cent of women work, representing the biggest gender gap of any ethnicity. Despite significant improvements in the educational attainment of girls of Bangladeshi origin and increases in the numbers of young women attending university, this is not reflected in improvements in labour market outcomes.

The women who participated in the review said that attitudes towards women's roles – both in their communities and nationwide – undermined their ability to participate socially and economically, even though most of them wanted to work and be financially independent. For those fortunate enough to find employment, Bangladeshi women in particular earn less than those from other ethnic minority groups. Although Muslim communities and society in general are becoming more progressive, some barriers and bigoted views remain and continue to impact the lives and opportunities of Muslim women.

Women still struggle to be respected and to control their own destinies in a male-dominated society, and Muslim women are confronted by extra hurdles, not least the misconception that their faith restricts them to taking on household roles. Despite the outmoded view that some people hold of Muslim women, there are many highly educated, independent and ambitious women who are ready and eager to make their mark. There is an untapped workforce here that could make a valuable contribution to the British economy. Yet the All Party Parliamentary Group on Race and Community reported that some Muslim women have even removed their hijab to increase their chances of finding work in what is supposed to be a cosmopolitan society, while others have removed themselves from the job market because of the discrimination they face.

Feeling accepted has a significant impact on Muslim women's ability and confidence to integrate into British society – and threats to deny or restrict minorities' identities undermine their commitment to a British national one. I am proud to be a product of multicultural Britain, but as a British-Bangladeshi Muslim, the biggest threat to my sense of British identity is Islamophobia, which is partly why I feel the need to defend the veil. To quote Hillary Clinton, 'Women's rights are human rights.' That applies to all women, whatever our faith, and in Britain in 2021, our right to freedom of religion shouldn't be in conflict with our ability to contribute to British society.

In April 2018, Ipsos MORI released a review regarding Muslim social attitudes. It showed that while young British Muslims are becoming more liberal, they are not becoming less religious. Muslim women have continued to educate and help people reassess their views of submission and oppression, both before and following the Brexit vote, but they have had a greater battle on their hands at a time when anti-immigrant sentiment is becoming normalised. As writer and journalist Aina Khan has pointed out, having to 'reassure people we are "good Muslims", not "Isis Muslims", is demoralising'.

On the positive side, many Muslim women from both the younger and older generations have challenged traditional stereotypes of Muslim womanhood portrayed by Western media through educational success, career choices and their roles in their homes and communities.

In my first job as a bilingual work experience coordinator for Tower Hamlets in 1992, I carried out a piece of research as to why many Bangladeshi and predominantly Muslim families were reluctant for their daughters to go to university after completing their A-levels. It was not that all families were against the idea; for many, it was simply the fear of the unknown. Would their daughters be accepted there? Would they cope? Would they be targets of discrimination? Would they ever return home? These were just some of the many questions raised. For some, there was also the fear of their daughters being in coeducational establishments and experiencing challenges in continuing to maintain the values and principles of the Islamic faith.

Over the past twenty-five years, the situation has been changing for British Muslim women, who have increasingly chosen career paths that depart from the traditional areas of tailoring or becoming teaching assistants. Shazia Mirza built her career as a stand-up comedian, actress and writer; Perween Warsi became a business professional and consultant; Unaiza Malik is a former treasurer of the Muslim Council of Britain; and Dr Zareen Roohi Ahmed, a philanthropist, entrepreneur, designer and community activist, has become a political voice for Muslims in the public sphere. These examples clearly show how British Muslim women have used their faith as a platform for politics, taking a stand in the public arena rather than being constrained.

For British Muslim women who have secured employment, this achievement is highly respected by their parents. Although it may seem superficial, a sense of 'keeping up appearances' is enormous here, with parents rivalling each other to see whose daughter has a higher salary, greater public standing and a better husband. At a women's event where I was the speaker, I could not help but laugh to myself as I listened intently to mothers competing with each other. They boasted about how their daughters got the best A-level results, who obtained a scholarship, whose daughter got into a Russell Group university, who passed their driving test first time, who had a mortgage and so on. In between eating samosas and meat biryani, each mother mentioned that a proposal like no other had arrived for their daughter, quietly showing me a potential groom on their phones and pretending to wipe the screen when their daughters hovered. When it was my turn to speak, I commended all of them and told them that I had been listening; that what it showed me is how far we have come to be proud that our daughters have achieved so much.

I had heard one of the mums say that she was getting an

Estée Lauder present for her daughter. I praised her and said that her daughter was lucky to have a mother who cared for her and appreciated how hard her daughter was working. I asked these mothers and daughters if they knew of Estée Lauder's famous words about success.

'I never dreamed about success. I worked for it.'

We must all work for success because dreaming alone will not deliver success. We can dream because that is what inspires us, but we have to do the hard slog, and for many of us it won't be an easy journey. Things might not work out the first time, but giving up is not an option. You can build your life by being courageous, travel the world on a budget, open your own business or go into politics.

To the daughters, I said, 'You can do all of this, but remember your mothers were with you, and you know they sacrificed things that they will not speak of. Remember them as you move on in life and live it standing up tall, proud and strong.'

Although Muslim women have faced greater challenges in breaking out of the traditional housewife mould, their active participation in different sectors of the workforce demonstrates how Islam gives equal rights to women, even in the choice of career. This once again dismisses the traditional image of Muslim womanhood. There are many powerful Muslim women in prominent positions who have overcome societal preconceptions to pursue their goals. One could argue that they have had to battle harder than many non-Muslim women to be accepted and valued, which is testament to their fortitude. Clearly, Muslim women are able to fight for equality but they need to be supported and celebrated to reach that equal platform – just like women all over the world.

There is much more that can and should be done to challenge stereotypes and build integration. Members of all parties, especially those in the ruling government, must eliminate all forms of racism from their thinking and rhetoric, including far-right populism. Trade unions also have a pivotal role to play in challenging racism and employing a zero-tolerance policy towards any form of discrimination. They need to create environments that promote cohesion and offer workable solutions to improve all employees' lives. Although the government and trade unions are fully aware that racism exists, they are not mind-readers and they don't have a crystal ball, so local and national politicians and trade union members need to build trust, encouraging people to talk in confidence and report issues of concern or incidents that they believe are racist. Tackling racism begins with empowerment but should result in penalties for all those who employ hate speech or are in breach of discrimination laws, without exception.

At the Stand Up to Racism rally at the London Muslim Centre in 2016, I delivered a speech about Muslim women, Islamophobia, universal human values and refugees. I spoke about the type of attitudes that Muslim women face from those who believe the stereotypes, but how despite ignorance you carry on, you become stronger, you learn, you move forward and you yourself can evolve as well. We should concentrate on the universal values that bind us together, not tear us apart.

CHAPTER 9

MEDIA, THE VEIL AND MUSLIM WOMEN

In September 2018, the *Wall Street Journal* published a controversial article by Andy Ngo titled 'A Visit to Islamic England', which claimed that multiculturalism in our capital has failed.

> My first visit was to Tower Hamlets, an East London borough that is about 38% Muslim, among the highest in the U.K. As I walked down Whitechapel Road, the *adhan*, or call to prayer, echoed through the neighborhood. Muslims walked in one direction for *jumu'ah*, Friday prayer, while non-Muslims went the opposite way. Each group kept its distance and avoided eye contact with the other … A sign was posted on a pole: 'Alcohol restricted zone.' … The scene could have been lifted out of Riyadh.

As his critics pointed out, it's a shame that Ngo felt compelled to share the benefit of his putative wisdom when it seems to have been gleaned from spending about half an hour in Tower Hamlets; quite apart from anything else, someone who had spent more time in the city might have realised that not making eye contact with strangers is less a sign of hostile segregation than a polite adherence to the Londoners' code. But perhaps Ngo knew this and opted not to share it with the *Wall Street Journal* reader, as he must surely have known that the alcohol restrictions on Whitechapel Road are not, as his article implies, imposed by the Muslim population but by the local council in order to combat antisocial behaviour.

Ngo began the article by describing how he felt on his first visit to an east London market in 2006 when he 'saw a group of women wearing head-to-toe black cloaks'. He said he 'froze, confused and intimidated by the faceless figures'.

These tropes matter, because, whether intentionally or not, they reinforce false stereotypes of both Muslim men and women; Muslim men being aggressive and abusive, and Muslim women being meek, subservient and oppressed. Although as a teenager Ngo found the Muslim women in 'cloaks' threatening, on his subsequent visit to London and first visit to Tower Hamlets he implied that these women were obedient, waiting outside the barbershop 'under the hot sun while their sons and husbands were groomed'.

In 2016, BBC Three screened the documentary *Is Britain Racist?* It featured niqab-wearing Muslim women being told to go back to where they came from, and a young woman who said that the common assumption made about Muslims is that 'all the men are terrorists, and all the women are at home feeding the terrorists'.

Although approximately 1.9 billion people in the world practise Islam, only a tiny extremist minority have skewed the teachings of the Quran to fit their own agenda. Nevertheless, the millions of law-abiding Muslims, who would agree that these terrorists are not true Muslims, are expected to apologise for the actions of a minority.

The media plays a significant role in shaping perceptions and attitudes, including those towards Muslims, who are frequently the subject of biased or even downright inaccurate reporting. Despite an IPSOS Mori poll finding that three quarters of people interviewed did not trust journalists, the fact remains that they still have the power to influence people. Research has shown that following the 9/11 tragedy, the British press began using a negative tone when talking about British Muslims, with the representation of Muslims in Western media only worsening after each subsequent terrorist attack.

Unfortunately, research has also shown that when controlling for other factors, such as number of fatalities, Muslim terrorist attacks seem to receive more media coverage than others. Therefore, when someone mentions the word 'terrorist', most people will picture someone Muslim.

Shortly after the Manchester attacks, I travelled to Rochester with my primary-aged son. When we boarded the train, we found spare seats in the middle of the carriage. After we sat down, the people near us moved away. I had a rucksack, and my son, whom I had collected from Arabic classes, was wearing the traditional white long shirt that Muslim men in the Middle East wear, together with his topi (hat). My son whispered to me, 'Do they think we are bad?' I pulled him closer and said, 'No, they don't think we are bad; they're just being silly.'

In 2016, the European Network Against Racism launched a project entitled 'Forgotten Women: the impact of Islamophobia on Muslim women' to document the disproportionate effect of Islamophobia on women and better address the intersectional discrimination they face. The published report showed that the media does not often consider Muslim women as having agency and depicts these women as either oppressed or dangerous, thereby failing to regard them as a diverse and heterogenous group.

Indeed, the British media has frequently propagated the idea that Muslim women are oppressed. According to the Centre for Feminist Foreign Policy, an analysis of 200 articles from eight of the most read newspapers in the United Kingdom over a one-year period (December 2015–December 2016) found that British newspapers perpetuate stereotypes of Muslim women as wives and mothers, as passive and submissive, and as victims and sex slaves. According to the 2018 report 'Misogyny, Racism, and Islamophobia: Street harassment at the intersections', veiled Muslim women are more at risk of street harassment because of their popular portrayal as culturally dangerous or threatening.

Like many Muslim women, I am brutally aware of

the impact of Islamophobia and the struggles that many law-abiding, peaceful British Muslims have faced since the increase in terrorism by people claiming to act in the name of Islam.

I was a teenager when Britain assisted America in the 1986 bombing of Libya. I recall with clarity standing at a bus stop as the only Muslim among my white schoolfriends. The bus driver shut the door in my face and told me to go back to Libya. I stood confused and dumbfounded while my friends banged on the window, screaming at the bus driver to stop and let me on the bus. As the bus drove off, I stayed there for some time, trying to fathom what I had done wrong. I managed to pull myself together, but with the humiliation of what the bus driver did to me, and with other white people watching me, silent tears began to fall down my cheeks. I don't know how I managed to walk home, because I could not feel my legs. On my journey, I met my father walking along the Delce Road looking for me. When I saw him, I ran to him and fell into his arms sobbing. At that point, I felt as though I wanted to shut myself indoors and never go out again. I felt as though the whole world knew what had happened and that everyone would be staring and pointing at me if I left the house. I felt sick and shaky and could not think about anything else. I replayed the incident over and over again in my mind.

It was then that I realised my faith (and my appearance) would be judged and would subject me to stereotyping and hostility for years to come. It was an odd feeling; a moment of brutal realisation that childhood toys and other trappings of safety and innocence would need to be put away as I graduated into an adult society of harsh judgements, false perceptions, harassment and discrimination.

There is an even darker side to this stereotyping. According to Aleksandra Dier, gender expert at the United Nations Security Council Counter-Terrorism Committee, terrorist groups such as ISIS have exploited these Western views by telling Muslim women that they can never be truly free to exercise their religion without stigma, without discrimination and without marginalisation in the West; that they will never be respected as Muslim women here. They are lured into joining the Caliphate with promises that they will be liberated from stigma, able to exercise their religion freely and live their lives as good Muslim women.

While newspaper coverage perpetuating stereotypes may have increased in the twenty years since 9/11, the marginalisation of Muslims in the media is not a new problem, nor is it simply a question of substandard news reporting. We do not need to look back many decades to see how foreign characters were stereotyped in TV series, many of which were comedies. *Mind Your Language*, for example, was a sitcom that aired between 1977 and 1986. It depicted stereotypes of non-English-speaking adults in a classroom setting. These students, from diverse backgrounds, had come to learn English; their lessons were given by a young white male teacher. The students included a Muslim man wearing a topi, a Sikh carrying a kirpan, an Indian woman in a sari who was always knitting, a German woman with blonde hair in plaits across the top of her head, a Japanese business-man with a camera around his neck and a flirtatious young French woman.

On one occasion, when I was waiting at the GP surgery with Mum so that I could interpret for her, a woman sat near us in the waiting area was knitting and kept smiling at us. She kept holding her knitting needles in the air, so we looked around, wondering why she was doing that. We then realised that she was waving them at us. Although I was a bit worried, the woman was smiling, so Mum gave a polite half-smile in return, clearly failing to understand why she needed to wave her knitting needles at us. The woman then proceed-ed to come over and sit with us, and asked Mum where her knitting needles were. Confused, Mum shook her head, so the woman laughed and said that she looked like the woman from *Mind Your Language*. She clearly assumed that knitting was what women like my mother did in their spare time.

Although it wasn't meant to offend, this assumption had been made based purely on the stereotypical portrayal of the Indian woman in the show. I have never forgotten this, as it made me realise that many people did not expect us to achieve anything outside the home environment; that they thought our role was purely to keep house, raise a family and knit. Perhaps the impact of this made me even more determined to prove to people that we are just as capable of pursuing successful careers in the corporate world as our white British counterparts.

In shaping popular views of Islam and Muslims, limited and stereotypical representation in the media not only affects how Muslim women engage with others and integrate with the wider community; it also has a serious impact on their access to job opportunities and maternity services, on their sense of security and on their human rights.

When my eldest child was born in 1995, my experience with the maternity services at the Royal London Hospital is one that I will never forget. I have since campaigned for their improvement. Though I didn't know it at the time, I was suffering from pre-eclampsia; the maternity appointments that might have diagnosed the condition always felt rushed, though I noticed that non-Bangladeshi women were given longer appointments. I asked the midwife why other pregnant women were having longer appointments and she snapped at me, saying that it was because they were experiencing problems.

This may well have been true, but in the group of Bangladeshi women attending the hospital with me there were several who had multiple health issues such as diabetes, high blood pressure and kidney problems. I know this because I had to interpret for some of the expectant mothers. One of the mothers who had diabetes was told that it was her fault and that she should stop eating sweet food. The midwife ignored the fact that both the woman's parents had diabetes, so it was probably hereditary. In the same conversation, she said that she had seen a programme about Bangladeshis which suggested that they ate sweet foods all the time and that's why they had diabetes. I pointed out that white people also often followed a main meal with a dessert like cake and custard. She wasn't happy with me and looked as though she wanted to send me to the back of the line like a naughty child. By that time, I had eaten three packets of crisps because I was so hungry!

The midwife told another woman that unless she stopped wearing a sari to her appointments, she would be seen last because it took her too long to get changed. However, the same midwife seemed to have plenty of time to spend with a white expectant mother wearing a smart suit to the clinic. I was instructed to tell one Muslim woman not to wear her scarf on her head when giving birth; I pointed out that when my mum gave birth, she had to wear a hospital cap.

As an expectant mum myself, I would sit for hours waiting to be seen and wonder why non-BME expectant mothers could waltz their way in so quickly. At the time, I was working for Bethnal Green City Challenge and my manager was good to me so didn't mind how long I took, although I had to ensure that my appointments were evidenced.

On the dirty wards, the staff made their lack of sympathy apparent, especially towards the Somali and Bangladeshi patients. The dreaded Mary Northcliffe Ward was where I spent over two weeks in April 1995, following the birth of my daughter, who weighed just under 5lb. On the same ward, there was a woman who had just had her second child. She was waiting to go home and when the midwife arrived with the paperwork to discharge her, she said, 'Mrs Begum, let's hope we don't see you here next year; it's not a hotel.' She went on to say, 'Your people don't know anything about contraception.' She claimed that she had seen documentaries on countries in the developing world not having access to such things.

It's shocking to think that this was only twenty-five years ago. While today the midwife concerned would probably be sacked and face prosecution, the sad fact is that these opinions still exist, even if people are no longer permitted to voice them publicly. Undoubtedly, this still creates barriers for women attempting to access health, recreation and community services, especially in places that are reluctant to meet their religious requirements.

Stigmatising and biased news reports not only affect how Muslim women are perceived but how they perceive the world in which they live. In one PhD study, the experiences of Muslim women engaging with UK maternity services were discussed, and showed how the women lacked confidence in discussing health concerns related to their religious practices. Some women stated that they had been reluctant to reveal that they had been fasting or intended to do so, for fear of judgement from staff. The impact of not divulging full medical details to a health practitioner could be significant, possibly resulting in misdiagnoses and the incorrect treatment of a patient.

Even those organisations that exist specifically to champion women's rights have tended to neglect Muslim women, so many have used social media to create their own Islamic feminist movements, such as #MosqueMeToo, to share their experiences of sexual harassment during the Hajj pilgrimage and in other religious settings. It is important for women to be able to relate to each other in order to minimise feelings of isolation. It seems ironic that organisations that promote women's rights should disregard Muslim women, yet there have been numerous investigations into racism in women's rights organisations such as Women Deliver, a group which alleges to champion gender equality and the health and rights of girls and women. In June 2020, an investigation was launched into allegations of racism and discrimination within the organisation. Staff complained of a toxic working environment and said the organisation suffered from a 'white saviour' complex. The CEO issued an apology and took a leave of absence until the investigation had been concluded.

In August 2020, *The Guardian* published an article about toxic racism within international women's rights groups. The author, Lori Adelman, vice-president at Global Fund for Women, who has worked with international feminist organisations for over a decade, said that racism is prevalent within the sector.

● ● ●

The Holocaust's most famous victim, Anne Frank, questioned the importance of words in her diary: 'Writing in a diary is a really strange experience for someone like me. Not only because I've never written anything before, but also because it seems to me that later on neither I nor anyone else will be interested in the musings of a thirteen-year-old schoolgirl.'

Little did she realise how powerful her words would be; that she would go on living even after her death, with her diary speaking poignantly to future generations.

Anne Frank is a positive example of the impact of words. It is words that conjure up images – good and bad – shape views and influence people. They say that actions speak louder than words, but sadly, the opposite is often true, with people quick to believe what others tell them, and the 'facts' often being distorted or even fabricated as the story travels from one person to another, or from one journalist to millions of readers.

But if words can propagate hate, they can also be used to spread love, tolerance and understanding. They can be used to promote communities coming together and the belief that even if you don't agree with someone's ideals, or subscribe to their beliefs, it does not mean that you should not respect them or live alongside them in harmony.

When I was hurt by the words of a bus driver all those years ago, my parents taught me that it is the way in which you respond and how you rise that will define how well you survive and progress in this world.

When I watch children's films with my daughters and my nieces, they immediately bring back childhood memories of fine and inclement weather, of sunny, pale blue skies or grey, stormy ones with the wind cutting through my starched school uniform. At that time, I longed to see someone like me in picture books or fashion magazines, on the TV or in cinemas. I walked up and down steep streets, catching my fingertips on thorns hidden among immaculate roses, brushing past perfectly pruned hedges, and through The Vines – Grade II-listed gardens in Rochester – laden with soft autumn leaves, without the slightest whisper of a sound. And all the time I looked for someone like me.

When I was younger, in the days when I longed to see people who looked like me in books and on TV and became mesmerised by the story of Pocahontas, I wanted desperately to see people like myself in authority. Now, when I look in the mirror, I see the reflection of someone who has stood up not only for herself, but for others who have been the minority for so long and whose voices have so often been ignored. I hope that I am now a role model to my children and others in my community. Today, we are working towards a nation where we see each other represented everywhere, but it's important that we accept our differences first. We are special as British, but we are also unique, and we are immensely proud of it.

These days, I am impressed by Muslim women who excel in roles that one has associated more with men, or white women. Sadia Asmat, for example, is a stand-up comedian from east London who plays on stereotypes to deliver lines such as, 'I'm comfortable covering my hair the same way you're comfortable covering your tits. And it's not for me to say you're oppressed by your top and your bra.'

A few weeks before writing this chapter, just prior to the first lockdown, my friend and younger daughter Nabila sat around my kitchen table for tea. As I laid the tea tray down and they moved their phones away, I spotted that they both had a picture of Pocahontas as their cover image; long flowing black hair, with a proud and defiant stance. Although she wasn't wearing a scarf, she still meant something to me, my friend and my daughter. She was a symbol of courage, of power, of making a crucial contribution to the world around her. She adapted to many difficult situations in an alien environment, but always succeeded.

And it is these strong definitive attributes of women – whatever their faith – that can inspire so many young Muslim women.

CHAPTER 10

THE COVID NIQAB

As we saw in earlier chapters, Muslim women who wear Islamic dress in Western countries are frequently subjected to verbal abuse and even physical attacks – but by far the worst harassment is reserved for those who choose to wear the niqab. The most conspicuous form of Islamic dress, the niqab is a face veil that only reveals the eyes. In general, it is worn with an abaya – a long, loose garment – and a hijab or headscarf. Although this type of dress is not required by Islam, it is recommended in some interpretations. In fact, the Quran does not insist on specific clothing for women but rather invites both men and women to behave with decency and integrity, both physically and morally. In Western society, it is very much a woman's personal choice.

A study entitled 'Behind the Veil: Why 122 women choose to wear the full face veil in Britain' revealed that nearly 80 per cent of wearers had experienced verbal and physical harassment. Often the abusers assumed that women wearing the niqab could not speak English, or that they were unlikely to retaliate. One of the women interviewed said, 'This lady was swearing at me; she was an old lady. And I told her, "You're like my grandma. Why are you swearing at me?" She was shocked and said, "Actually, I didn't know you could speak."'

Another woman said that other common insults and questions included 'Ninja', 'Go back to where you came from', 'Are you going to blow me up?' and 'Is there a bomb underneath there?'

As these examples show, most perpetrators perceive niqab-wearing women as oppressed, stupid, outsiders or a threat. Nearly 80 per cent of the respondents in the above study said that their abusers were predominantly white. The abuse came from both genders, but men were more often the abusers and tended to be more aggressive or violent.

I believe that this is partly due to the pervasive hostility towards Muslims that is encouraged by the right-wing media and, clearly, it happens more often to women who are visibly Muslim. But it's not just individual perpetrators: this kind of prejudice and discrimination appears on an institutional level too – as Kulsuma Begum knows first-hand. Begum, a mother of four, was prevented from entering her son's primary school because she wears the niqab. The school's visitor policy banned it. She was not the only mum who was affected. As she was not a school governor, she did not have authorisation to be present at policy change meetings. As a result, she started a campaign and leaders from

Women100, an east London community initiative, took up her cause, which they saw as a justice issue. Eventually, after seven months, the school changed its visitor policy.

In much of Europe, the situation is even worse, with institutional intolerance extending to a state ban on wearing the niqab or burqa in public in a number of countries. France introduced a total public ban in April 2011, followed by Belgium in July 2011. More outrageously, as we saw in Chapter 6, in 2016 some French local mayors attempted to outlaw burkinis – modest swimwear that does not conceal the wearer's face. Bulgaria, the Netherlands and Latvia imposed the burqa ban in 2016, followed by Austria in 2017 and Denmark in 2018 (though it has been widely reported that in the Netherlands at least the law proved unworkable as the Dutch police and transport companies expressed their unwillingness to enforce it).

Even more shockingly, in the Netherlands a woman covering her face with a veil in public buildings including schools and hospitals, and on public transport, can be fined €150 and denied access to public spaces, yet anyone found in possession of a small amount of drugs for personal use will generally not be prosecuted. What sort of signal does this send to Muslim women about the relative threat they're assumed to pose to the country?

Yet in 2020 it became mandatory in all of these countries, along with many others, to wear a face mask in certain public places for protection against Covid-19. Will their governments make Muslim women wear one type of face mask for public health reasons but forbid them to wear another type of face mask for cultural and religious reasons, even if they are made from the same material?

The motivations for banning the full-face veil, according to the Parliamentary Assembly of the Council of Europe when in 2010 it sought to legitimise the niqab ban in European countries, are to avoid sex discrimination, inequality and infringement of European cultural norms, and to promote public safety, national security and national cohesion. These arguments seemed weak enough then, given that the ban is an infringement of several key human rights, including freedom of thought, conscience and religion, freedom of expression and freedom from discrimination. As most women who wear the veil do so out of choice, it is unclear how banning it might help to protect women from sex discrimination. In addition, 'European cultural norms' have changed vastly over the years, with most European countries embracing multiculturalism. Is there a fundamental set of European norms, and if so, who decides what these are?

In light of the coronavirus pandemic, the arguments appear even weaker. Because non-Muslims are now deemed to benefit, suddenly national security is no longer under threat from people covering their faces.

While the previous ruling violated Muslim women's freedom of expression and personal choice, everyone else is now permitted to choose the type of mask they wish to wear, from plain to colourful; from small to large. Even President

Macron turned up at a school in May 2020 wearing a navy mask embellished with the French flag.

The irony of banning burqas while making face masks compulsory has not escaped critics around the world. Fatima Khemilat, a fellow at the Political Science Institute of Aix-en-Provence, said:

> If you are Muslim and you hide your face for religious reasons, you are liable to a fine and a citizenship course where you will be taught what it is to be 'a good citizen'. But if you are a non-Muslim citizen in the pandemic, you are encouraged and forced as a 'good citizen' to adopt 'barrier gestures' to protect the national community.

London-based lawyer Satvinder Juss said:

> Suddenly, with Covid-19, states are saying that they need to have facial masks. So out through the window go all arguments about the right to look into people's faces and around integration. It becomes impossible now to defend this. The whole of the lower part of the face is covered by a mask, which is the same with the niqab.

Will the wearing of these masks damage community relations, which was one of the reasons they gave for implementing the burqa ban? Hardly. Masks or not, the world seems to be communicating effectively during this crisis.

The executive director of Human Rights Watch, Kenneth

Roth, tweeted in May 2020: 'Can the Islamophobia be any more transparent? The French government mandates masks but still bans the burqa.'

How does a face mask to help protect against coronavirus differ from a niqab? Both are worn for a specific purpose, in public, but neither are worn 24/7. Some Muslims are proud to show their faith by wearing the niqab in public, whereas a highly infectious disease requires everyone to wear face masks in public buildings and in situations where they are in close proximity to other people. The wearing of face masks also demonstrates good manners and respect for other people, in the same way as maintaining a social distance of two metres does. If we all start wearing masks routinely, does this mean that we are being subservient by following government directives? Does it inhibit our communication? Herein lies the hypocrisy of the argument against face coverings.

Of course, a small but vocal minority would argue that we are being subservient – or, as they might put it, 'sheep' – by wearing masks. Some people to whom I have spoken have said that they have been called 'paranoid' by non-mask wearers. Others have been criticised for following government guidelines and giving people a wide berth in public and have been subjected to statements such as 'We don't have coronavirus, you know'. According to a BBC report, men are more likely to refuse to wear masks than women, even though more men die from Covid-19. But the mask-refusers and conspiracy theorists are a tiny proportion of the population; in general, the British public have strongly supported measures to combat coronavirus, in spite of the culture shock it has entailed for some.

The mandatory wearing of face masks was a new experience for many people who were used to conveying their feelings through facial expressions. Some people said that their eyes ached from creasing them more when smiling at people to compensate for their mouths being covered. However, the main form of communication is speech, so in that sense nothing has changed, except perhaps having to speak a bit louder to be heard.

Now that face masks have become the norm, many Muslim women say that public life has become less threatening. In many fashion stores, we are seeing a range of stylish, washable face masks as an alternative to the scratchy disposable masks that are handed out in hospitals. What used to attract controversy for Muslim women has now become a fashion statement, albeit for different reasons.

But why has it taken a global pandemic for face coverings to become widely accepted? After all, Covid aside, we are all able to walk into a public building in the cold winter months wearing woolly hats with half our faces hidden by scarves, and we do not view these as inhibiting reciprocity and communication. In many situations and professions, it is standard practice for people to cover their faces all year round: surgeons, dentists, ice hockey players, skiers, motorcyclists and so on. Although these coverings are removed when these professions or sports are not being practised, they do not incite the same fear, judgement or even hatred as Muslim coverings when they are being worn. It's not, therefore, the covering that is an issue but the stereotypes that people associate with it.

Lauren Booth, a journalist who converted to Islam in 2010, has suggested that there is an idea among some in the West that banning the niqab will end terrorism. It may not be entirely conscious, but the fervour in some European countries for banning visible signs of Muslim faith suggests they see a clear link between practising your religion by dressing modestly and becoming a terrorist – which, needless to say, is profoundly upsetting to many Muslims.

What is certainly true is that, regardless of the motivation behind it, the end result of the burqa ban is that Muslim women are penalised for expressing their religious and personal choices. This is Islamophobia. The Equality and Human Rights Commission says that a ban 'which only applies to some religious symbols or dress but not others would be unlawful direct discrimination'. The logical conclusion is that any country that wishes to ban the niqab and burqa should also ban any other form of religious attire, including Sikh turbans, Jewish kippahs and Catholic nuns' veils. The fact that such a move would be unthinkable should tell us something about how far these countries are really motivated by a 'commitment to upholding secular values'.

It also speaks volumes about how far these restrictions encroach on our human rights – and the effects have been severe. A 2019 study by the Economic Research Forum found that after the French National Assembly banned conspicuous religious symbols in schools in 2004 (a law predominantly affecting Muslim girls), the attainment gap between Muslim and non-Muslim girls more than doubled. Of course, this gap then continues into adulthood, harming economic and social integration in the long term. Professor Agnès De Féo, who has studied the effects of the 2010 burqa ban, argues that it has 'created a monster', fuelling Islamophobia and further entrenching divisions in French society: 'Those who have left to go and fight in Syria say that this law is one of the things that encouraged them. They saw it as a law against Islam. It had the effect of sending a message that Islam was not welcome in France.'

In October 2018, the UN Human Rights Committee found that the ban disproportionately and unnecessarily affected Muslim women's right to practise their religion and, rather than protecting women, 'could have the opposite effect of confining them to their homes, impeding their access to public services and marginalising them'. It will come as no surprise in the Covid era, but the committee was 'not persuaded by France's claim that a ban on face covering was necessary and proportionate from a security standpoint or for attaining the goal of "living together" in society'.

Even if it were considered a proportionate security measure, it clearly isn't effective at achieving its stated goal: a 2019 study in the *Journal of European Public Policy* found that countries imposing restrictions on wearing the veil saw an increase, rather than a decrease, in terrorist attacks.

On 11 April 2011 in France, under Nicolas Sarkozy's administration, it became illegal to wear the full-face veil in public. However, in October 2019, President Macron warned against linking the Islamic religion with terrorism, and called for a better understanding of the Muslim faith in France. And yet in the same month, a Muslim mother who was on a school trip with her son to the regional parliament in Bourgogne-Franche-Comté received verbal abuse from the chamber and was asked to remove her headscarf – even though it was prohibited neither by French law nor by the rules of the chamber. In response, President Macron warned against stigmatising Muslims – though the burqa ban does precisely that.

Muslim women who opt to wear the niqab do so out of personal choice, in the same way that all women are free to choose what they wish to wear. Our choices are a sign of individuality, not statements of 'separation and difference' as Jack Straw suggested in 2006 in a comment that naturally sparked anger among the Muslim community and fuelled discrimination.

While the singling out of Muslim women has made life very difficult for them, the debate about the niqab has changed, as has that of the veil. In 2006, Jack Straw could not have envisaged a world in which we would all have to wear masks to protect ourselves and others from Covid-19.

I agree that there are situations where it is necessary to remove the niqab, such as emergency medical situations or where there is a legitimate security concern. Nevertheless, in the current Covid-19 era, would a Muslim courtroom attendee be expected to remove her niqab when it is mandatory to wear a face mask?

I appreciate that very human instinct to want to see someone's face when having a conversation, as we pick up cues from their expressions, which is difficult when a woman is wearing a niqab. And yet there are other situations where we have conversations with people whom we cannot see, such as radio interviews and telephone calls; and our human instinct accepts this. This has become even more commonplace over the past year, not only when we are unable to meet someone in person, but because we all have to wear masks and social distance. It is possible that this will become the cultural norm, which may seem absurd to some, but is something that has long been practised in other parts of the world out of consideration for others.

By removing Muslim women's prerogative to wear what they please, a ban not only denies them freedoms that are allowed to others; it also pushes their voices and lived experiences out of the mainstream and into the margins, isolating them from society.

Once, during a personal and social education tutorial in my sixth form, our tutor asked if there was a book that any of us would like the group to look at. It was just before Nelson Mandela was due to be released from prison. No one suggested a book, so I proposed that we read *The Autobiography of Malcolm X*, which was originally published in 1965. The class went quiet; clearly, it wasn't the sort of book my white classmates read. When we came to discuss it, one white girl said she couldn't read the whole book because she just didn't understand or connect to it and she didn't see why she should be forced to read it.

I still remember what I felt listening to her words: a shooting pain hitting a part of my identity that had been hurt repeatedly. And yet that part of me continued to get up and keep going. I replied that I'd had to read things to which I couldn't relate my entire life, but that I found a way regardless, because a fundamental part of learning is trying to understand other people's perspectives.

For as long as I can remember when I was growing up, I was taught about the achievements of white people, particularly white men. If you have never experienced or considered how detrimental it is or could be to grow up without role models who reflect or connect to you in every situation and establishment – school, the media, industry, government and so on – then you have a sense of white privilege.

Pushing Muslim women's voices and preferences aside not only has a negative impact on those who are silenced; it also denies others the opportunity to learn from new perspectives and benefit from our strengths.

A Bangladeshi Muslim friend of mine, Rukiya, whom I met some years after I moved to Tower Hamlets, never wore the scarf growing up, had dyed blonde hair, wore high heels and was often in trouble for truanting from school. Rukiya later began wearing the scarf and eventually wore the niqab. She was highly articulate and became a legal rights adviser.

We were once in her car, trying to negotiate parked cars outside a school. It was our right of way, and a lorry coming in the opposite direction had to wait for the line of traffic to pass through. I thought Rukiya might be courteous and allow the lorry driver through, even though it wasn't his right of way. However, she wasn't having any of that. The burly driver saw Rukiya approaching and, while he seemed happy to let the other cars go by, he moved out and tried to squeeze past her. It was a stand-off. It seemed as though we were sat there for ages while the driver and a niqab-wearing Muslim woman had a stare-down challenge. The driver got out of his cab, strode towards us and stood in front of the car with his arms crossed.

Rukiya is an incredibly stubborn and resilient woman, having endured a great deal in her life, so she will not back down if someone tries to pull a fast one on her.

Rukiya got out and marched over to the man. She looked at him and folded her arms across her chest in defiance. By this time, the altercation had attracted the attention of mums dropping off their children at school. There were two elderly white women with their shopping trolleys staring at the scene as they whispered among themselves.

'All right love, now you need to move your little piece,' said the lorry driver.

'Oh, right, you want me to move my little piece. What are you fucking gonna do if I don't move my piece?' screamed Rukiya from behind her veil in her Cockney accent.

The white man's mouth dropped as he took a step back. 'What the fuck?'

'Don't you "what the fuck" with me; you move *your* piece out of the way.'

'And what about if I don't?' asked the man, scratching his head. Clearly it was the first time he'd had to deal with a Muslim woman in a niqab screaming at him in the middle of the road.

'I got all the time in the world to stand here while we both sweat it out,' Rukiya said, as she leaned back on her car.

The beeping of other cars was increasingly becoming louder, as drivers became impatient, and a young man with a beard shouted out to the white man: 'Mate, please, just move on and listen to her.'

The white lorry driver looked back at the young man with the beard and back to Rukiya. The mums watched, the two shoppers watched, and there was tension in the air. Everyone looked at the lorry driver, awaiting his response. I glanced anxiously around from the passenger seat, praying that there was no journalist nearby!

The bearded young man pleaded: 'I've got a wife like her at home and they don't give in. I'm already late getting home, and she won't be pleased.'

Rukiya gave him a venomous glance.

Then a Bangladeshi mum from the other side of the road screamed, 'Moove! Move!'

This encouraged a chorus of 'Move!' from the other mothers, while a teacher walked past the gates pretending she hadn't noticed anything.

One of the elderly white women hobbled over, while her

friend looked after her shopping trolley and stood next to Rukiya.

She looked up at the lorry driver and said, wagging her finger, 'Oy! Get on your bike and fuck off.'

Just as my friend boldly stood up to the white lorry driver, so women of all faiths and backgrounds – whether they wear the niqab or not – need to stand up for their rights, continue to defy stereotypes and fight for equality, so that they may become the role models that many of us never had as children.

PART FOUR

A BRITAIN FOR ALL WOMEN — VEILED AND UNVEILED

CHAPTER 11

CONTEMPORARY MUSLIM WOMEN – SUCCEEDING THROUGH SETBACKS

If life as a Muslim woman in Britain teaches you anything, it's that you shouldn't be fazed by other people's misperceptions of you – although sometimes it's difficult not to be surprised by them.

I had been a councillor in Tower Hamlets for a few years and had got used to facing down all the usual myths and legends, whether it was that Muslim women belong at home, not in public life, or that as a woman I was 'easily controlled' by men, when, after reading some particularly searing comments about me on Facebook, I went to my local Sainsbury's to pick up some groceries. As I walked around the aisles, I became aware of two Bangladeshi women following me around. I smiled at them and one of them shyly came up to me and asked in Bengali if I was Rabina Khan. I said yes.

She called her friend over excitedly and they both asked if they could take a selfie with me.

After they'd both taken selfies with me, in several different poses, they smiled and asked what I was doing in Sainsbury's. When I explained that I was shopping for groceries, they looked surprised and asked why. I told them that I needed food to cook dinner for my children.

'Do you actually cook?'

I nodded. Concerned, they asked, 'Don't you have a maid? And where is your driver?'

Trying to contain my amusement, I replied, 'Not everyone has help at home, and my driver is my husband outside waiting for me.'

Back in Bangladesh, they had seen politicians with maids and personal chauffeurs, so assumed that I was like this.

Although I was already a Labour Party member, it wasn't until 2010 that I decided to become more actively involved in politics. My decision to do so was based on my determination to fight for the rights of my entire community – whatever their nationality, background, or problem – and choosing the political route seemed to be the best platform from which to achieve this. This was entirely my own decision and was not influenced by my parents, friends or colleagues, even though they supported my choice. All of my previous roles were centred around mentoring people with a diverse range of issues and problems – whether it was racism, domestic violence or housing issues – representing their rights and helping disenfranchised young people. My work then and my subsequent pivot to politics were both fuelled by my family's experiences of racism, false judgement and isolation. In 2010 I was elected to stand in Shadwell ward with two other Labour candidates. The ward I had been selected for was one that few thought I would win, not least because it had normally been won by male candidates. Though Shadwell had been a solidly Labour ward since 1919, in 2007, it had been won by Respect, an anti-war and anti-privatisation party.

Before the 2010 elections, Tower Hamlets Council had approximately three male councillors for every woman. Not only was I swimming against the tide as a woman, but when the election campaign kicked off, I was also pregnant with my youngest child – and that was a first for a long time in Tower Hamlets Council. I began knocking on doors, along with a couple of volunteers; as Shadwell was not a target seat, most of our campaigners were sent elsewhere. In the first week, I campaigned in Shadwell Gardens, a huge estate comprising council flats, leaseholders and privately renting tenants. Word had got around that a Muslim woman in a hijab was standing for the Labour Party in Shadwell. Under a dreary sky, I met a small group of Bangladeshi men, three of them middle-aged and two younger, who began to congregate around the football pitch on the estate. They were whispering, smoking and laughing loudly. Initially, I could not assign to them any obvious political affiliation, but I just felt that they were doubtful about the ability of a slight Muslim woman to be a successful politician.

The grey rainclouds wrapped themselves around the estate as I walked down the steps of the block of flats adjacent to the group. I almost slipped walking out through the entrance, where the damaged doors had previously been removed. I could hear a burst of laughter erupt from the group and one of the men shouted out: 'This is a Respect strong area, and the Labour Party sent a Muslim woman knowing she will lose.'

Ignoring them, I looked at my clipboard with my colleague, as one of the younger men shouted: 'You should go home, have a cup of tea and look after the family. It's not worth it here; you will lose.'

With that, thunderous laughter emanated from the group and they slapped each other on the back as though they had already won the election. Their mirth echoed in my ears and I steeled myself with curled lips and got back to work.

With my growing belly, and the support of my close and extended family, I continued to knock on doors, talking to local families about the policies that could help advocate for their housing, education and community rights, and letting them know that I would run regular surgeries. Rather than relying on the Labour Party mantra, I drew on my experiences of being a governor for two different schools, having been a recent writer-in-residence at a girls' school, and having had articles published for the BBC London community pages, which were based at Rich Mix, the arts centre in Shoreditch, at the time. As I went from house to house, women opened doors and peeped from beneath the corner of a sari or a veil. They seemed fascinated to see a woman, after so many years, asking how they felt and what they dreamed of for their children. And it was the women who fascinated me, for suddenly they wanted to talk to me about their stories of struggle and fear. I think it was the fact I had taken the time to ask them what they needed, feared and hoped for. It was reciprocated, for they began to talk to their children, families and friends about me. I stood at the school gates conversing with mothers and their children, and walked through the market listening to people and signposting them to services.

One day, I met a group of older Bangladeshi men coming out of one of the mosques. One of them saw me, chuckled and called me over.

I walked over, unsure of what they would say to me. I prepared for the inevitable: being told that I would lose and I should go home and look after my family. With a crinkly smile under a wiry silver beard, this gentleman stood with his nodding group dressed in their long white tunics and intricate caps. I smiled and offered the Islamic salutations of Salaam humbly and said, 'Uncle, how are you? How can I help?' It is culturally respectful to refer to older men and women as uncles and aunts.

They roared with laughter, and with a sense of 'Here we go again', I felt uneasy. I smiled politely and waited.

'So, you are standing in the election?' he asked loudly, attracting more older men to crowd around him.

Another man with henna-dyed hair, a beard, bushy salt

and pepper brows and a black walking stick bore his eyes into my face and said, 'Are you strong enough to do this?'

They all looked at me and the crowd grew, waiting for my response as I struggled to hold my veil in place against the wind. The Islamic scent of musk from the circle of men was making my head explode. At other times, it would have not mattered, but pregnancy has that effect. Instead of focusing on the memory of the group of men who had jeered at me previously, I thought about all those who were keen to share their stories with me because I connected with them on a personal level. They viewed me differently to those campaigners who had no concept of the daily struggles they faced, and they found comfort in backing someone who could ensure that their voices were heard.

Almost thirty faces looked at me, and I wondered what test this was, but nothing can be won without winning hearts and minds.

'I am standing in the election, and I am strong – but I am stronger if you are all with me. Are you with me?' I looked at them with my head held high.

There was a prolonged silence. They looked at me and smiles began to break out among them. Then their leader clapped his hands.

'You have my vote. Maybe I don't have a choice; my wife has been talking about you!'

An almighty cheer of delight hailed me as their candidate to win. Word soon got around that Rabina was not going to be a pushover.

The only problem during the campaign was that, at four months pregnant, I could not stop eating! At the time, Percy Ingle Bakery in Watney Market had an eating area where I would recuperate between walking up and down steps and in and out of lifts, dodging groups of men, lugging hundreds of scrappy thin leaflets around and shoving them through letter boxes, avoiding any snappy dogs biting my fingers in the process. Pat from Percy Ingle always made sure I had a hot cup of tea and a pastry before I started an evening's campaign session.

In May 2010, at the Mile End count, I won the election in Shadwell by just three votes.

I felt privileged to win a seat so long occupied by men. Unequal representation, particularly an absence of women from ethnically diverse backgrounds, can mean a lack of advocacy for issues important to women of colour and a lack of opportunity to empower underserved communities. Some women find it easier to relate to other women than to men and feel more comfortable sharing their struggles with a female politician, as I have discovered. Little did I know that the next four years would be both incredibly difficult and deeply rewarding.

My son, Yameen, was born in November 2010. I was a first-time councillor, nursing a newborn and getting to grips with a Cabinet position I'd been given just a month earlier. Having supported Lutfur Rahman's successful bid to become Labour's mayoral candidate for Tower Hamlets, I continued to back him when he was later removed by

Labour's National Executive Committee and replaced with another candidate. Rahman stood as an independent in the mayoral election that October and won – and I became the Cabinet Member for Housing. I was delighted to take on this position, as I was already aware of the many challenges surrounding the provision of affordable housing and the effect that it had on Tower Hamlets' residents. Yet I was apprehensive, for housing was a dire problem for so many; I never could have envisaged the amount of casework, unpicking housing policies and finding a way to secure funding for housing that would consume my time. Balancing this hugely demanding portfolio with a baby, a primary-aged child and an adolescent, and constantly batting away opposition attacks, forced me to be strong. To never crumble or permit people, particularly white men, to make me feel small and undermined.

Now, just before Christmas, I found myself breastfeeding my son and working with the director for housing on a bid for the government's Decent Homes funding so that the borough's council homes could have new kitchens and bathrooms.

Yameen was a month old when I took up my council responsibilities. Council meetings often continued until late at night. Exhausted, I sat there facing the onslaught of the opposition councillors, listening to the accusations, heckling and sarcastic laughter. In the early days, my mum looked after my son for me in the Cabinet room and I snatched some time during any intervals to breastfeed in the ladies' prayer room. When he was a few weeks older, I would slip away to express milk quickly.

I worked hard to make a success of the portfolio, made friends and collaborated with people. Over time, my councillor surgery became very busy. It was a pleasure to try to help so many local residents by addressing the issues they were facing, whether it was housing problems or legal issues, schooling and so on, and I felt privileged to be involved in major improvement projects, even though it was arduous at times.

However, there was a dark side to being a councillor whose contact details were publicly available.

From the moment I began serving as a Cabinet member, the anonymous phone calls began. There were threats to my children, including one where the caller said he would make a Milly Dowler story out of my daughters, referring to the tragic case in which a thirteen-year-old girl on her way home from school was abducted, raped and murdered. Another said he had just followed me home; his account of how I had collected my son from nursery and pushed him home in his buggy was alarmingly accurate. I reported the call to the police, and the following day, special police officers checked the nursery facilities. These threats continued on a regular basis but increased dramatically during election periods. After the 2014 elections, a man used a pillar from our front garden to push our front door open and then ran off. During the 2018 mayoral elections, a man attempted to enter my home under the pretence of delivering food. My daughter and I pushed the door back to prevent him from entering. We were two slight women pushing against the weight of a large, sturdy man, but it's amazing how self-preservation enables you to find strength that you didn't know you had. We felt shaken afterwards, but were proud that we had stood up against someone who was three times our size.

In 2014, I was re-elected to the council, this time as a Tower Hamlets First candidate. The party pledges included building more affordable homes, reducing poverty, increasing aspirations and educational achievement, creating safer streets, tackling air pollution and providing better care for elderly residents – issues dear to my heart. I campaigned just as I had in 2010 when I first stood. I knocked on doors and made sure that I connected to the people I wished to represent again. As mentioned previously, in a borough as diverse as Tower Hamlets, I had the ability to connect to residents from different ethnic backgrounds, and being bilingual was a distinct advantage, particularly when communicating with Bengali residents whose first language was not English. This time, I won with a bigger margin than previously against Labour rivals.

In 2015, Tower Hamlets Council was at the centre of political controversy; Mayor Lutfur Rahman was removed from office by the courts following allegations that he had breached electoral rules, and a new election was held. It was a challenging and upsetting time, trying to understand what went wrong, and I was in shock when the court found Rahman guilty. Naturally, there were consequences for the other party members. I was judged as being guilty by association, even though I had absolutely no knowledge of any electoral fraud. But I've been taught that it isn't just our own actions and words that define us, but how we deal with the events around us. Some people crumble, whereas others view setbacks as stepping stones and emerge more determined. As author and personal growth expert Robin S. Sharma said: 'There are no mistakes in life, only lessons. There is no such thing as a negative experience, only opportunities to grow, learn and advance along the road of self-mastery. From struggle comes strength. Even pain can be a wonderful teacher.'

In June 2015, I stood as an independent candidate in the Tower Hamlets mayoral by-election, running against Labour's candidate, John Biggs. The media described me as a 'strong contender', with *The Guardian* reporting: 'Labour strategists are nervous … If Biggs wins, it will be a huge relief to him and to Labour in the East End. If Khan wins, it will be sensational.' With only three weeks to prepare, drawing on very limited resources compared with my mainstream rivals and facing intense opposition from all three of the major parties, the pressure was on.

There were comical moments, though, not least at my campaign launch at the Waterlily in Tower Hamlets. My brother Joynal came to support me – or at least he tried to. The building was packed out with people and it felt as though the world's media were there. There were stewards every-where, and when my brother tried to get in, they stopped him, saying the building had reached capacity. Joynal told them he was my brother. They just laughed, and it was only when he insisted that the steward pulled up a picture of me on his phone and held it up to compare me to my brother.

Joynal stood there waiting for the assessment while the steward scratched his head, looking from my brother's face to mine and discussing me with his colleague.

Impatiently, my brother pulled out his phone and showed our family pictures; that's when he was allowed in. When we spoke in the hall and he told me how he had got through my two bodyguards at the front entrance, I burst into laugh-ter, attracting the attention of nearby journalists. I had just made an emotional speech and then along comes my broth-er to tell me that security had given him clearance only after he'd proved his credentials by showing our family photos.

But there were also very difficult times, with the oppo-sition parties in Tower Hamlets, and particularly Labour, attempting to paint me as corrupt because I had served under Mayor Rahman in the controversial previous admin-istration. In the run-up to the election, I was described as 'a Rahman puppet' by John Biggs and as a 'stooge candidate for Rahman' by other critics. However, the line that always followed these accusations was: 'Ms Khan has no allegations against her.'

To counter these smears, I made sure that I accepted as

many media interviews as I could. While the journalists were generally more interested in the court case than in my campaign, I was determined to share my story of being an independent Muslim woman standing in an election against a mainstream party at an incredibly toxic time. I pointed out that I became a candidate not because I was a convenient puppet for anyone but because a huge majority of Bangladeshi community leaders, writers and journalists thought I would make an effective mayor.

I drew on my record as councillor, noting that I was the first Muslim woman to hold the portfolio for Housing and Regeneration and that from 2010 to 2015 I was instrumental in the creation of more than 4,500 new homes in Tower Hamlets. I had been involved in key regeneration projects, including the Ocean Estate Regeneration Project, which won the *Sunday Times* award for most improved borough, and the Whitechapel Vision, which won a national Planning Award. I'd had a leading role on the Blackwall Regeneration Initiative, helped secure Poplar Housing Zone and also won the Andy Ludlow Homelessness Award for managing homelessness in the borough. My manifesto spoke of transparency and accountability; housing and regeneration; employment and enterprise; education and young people; community safety and cohesion; health and wellbeing; environment and public space; and arts, culture and heritage. It wasn't just words on paper; I made myself available in person to listen to people's concerns and champion their causes. One of my supporters said in a newspaper article, 'Whenever people go to her for help, she helps them', while another said:

> We've had lots of politicians who say they represent the community but whom you only see at elections. We prefer politicians who are on the front line, actively involved on the ground. It will also be very good to get a woman elected and break through all the sexism. And Rabina Khan is a champion of fighting racism and promoting diversity in Tower Hamlets.

Rather than just paying lip service to key areas that needed to be tackled, I made pledges that I knew were achievable. I did not wish to waste time condemning the opposition, as that was not what people wanted to hear; they wanted to know what I could do for them. I aimed to challenge unfair decisions that affected the lives of people from all walks of life by fighting to retain free homecare and adult social care, tackling racism, campaigning for equal pay where a woman is doing equal or similar work, advocating for fairer leasehold charges and opposing the 'bedroom tax' – a tax imposed on residents renting a property with a spare bedroom.

I remember knocking on a door in Stepney and a well-built white woman with a face covered in rosacea opening the door. Her arms were folded defensively when I introduced myself to her. I spotted a newspaper on the floor and

A BRITAIN FOR ALL WOMEN

wondered if she had read about me. I said I hoped she would consider voting for me.

I took a step back and then she shouted, 'You're Rabina, ain't you?'

I nodded like a robot. My heart sank at the tone of her voice. I braced myself for a tirade of abuse, assuming that she had already judged me based on what she had read.

'Oh my gawd!' she said. 'Course I'm gonna vote for you. 'Cause of you, I got a roof over my head.'

She went on to explain: 'We ain't never met, babe. I emailed you last year 'cause of the bedroom tax and you sorted it. It helped me downsize from me old flat. Couldn't stay in the three bedrooms after me mum had died, 'cause of the rent.'

It's those moments that helped overshadow the relentless negativity on social media. Bizarrely, although the mainstream media began to view me more favourably during the election, the insults from the opposition on social media became more brutal, particularly from white men who blogged about me as though they knew everything about me, when in reality they knew nothing at all. It seems a lot easier for some to hide behind a computer screen and be gratuitously offensive on social media than to write a thoughtful, balanced article.

But despite all the slurs and the toxic campaigning, I managed to inspire more than 25,000 people to vote for me as their first preference, coming a close second to Labour on

27,000, with the Conservatives a distant third on less than 6,000.

Of course it was hugely disappointing to come so close and then fall short, but one of the lessons I learned from that election was the importance of carrying on with determination after a setback, daunting as it feels at the time. When I had to return as the loser to the council chambers following the election, it felt difficult to listen to the goading of the opposition. But as Mahatma Gandhi said, 'They cannot take away our self-respect if we do not give it to them.' I never allow anyone to take my self-respect.

So how did I cope with defeat?

Well, one thing that helped a lot was spending time talking to constituents, especially while consuming large quantities of food! A local café called the Hungry Cow kept me fed and topped up with tea, and as we know in the East End, a cuppa does a lot of good. It was ordinary folk who said to me, 'Rabina, go back and do what you enjoy' – and for me that was supporting people in my casework, challenging things that were not right and campaigning for change. I also knew that I had a responsibility to connect, engage and inspire, challenging the misperceptions that still abound regarding Muslim women.

We often learn greater lessons in adversity than we do in victory. Adversity is a test of character, endurance and courage. It can equip us with the motivation we need to inspire change and pursue our dreams. It also helps us to show more compassion and tolerance and to become less judgemental.

Setbacks are inevitable, but we can choose how we react to them.

TV chef and author Nadiya Hussain rose to fame in 2015 after winning the BBC's *Great British Bake Off*. As a child, she had endured sexual abuse and racist bullying, and the debilitating anxiety and panic attacks that followed continued into adulthood. While competing in the *Bake Off*, she was suffering from panic attacks in her hotel room after the day's filming – and her success brought with it daily racist abuse on social media. She admitted struggling initially with her public identity being so strongly associated with being Muslim: 'I certainly didn't enter a baking show in the hope of representing anyone. Being a Muslim for me was incidental, but from the day the show was launched, I was "the thirty-year-old Muslim" and that became my identity.' But despite all this, she is pursuing a rewarding and high-profile career and, to date, has written nine books. She dismisses toxic comments as being 'in the minority' and has also used her Twitter account to educate her followers about Ramadan. When she won the competition, her words struck a chord with many viewers: 'I am never going to put boundaries on myself ever again. I'm never going to say I can't do it. I can. And I will.'

The difference for successful people is that they do not view setbacks as the end of the story. Nadiya serves as an inspiration to others by talking openly about her struggles in the hope that it will reduce the stigma associated with mental illness and show people with anxiety disorders that they still have the power to achieve great things. She has used her position in the public eye to help people and raise awareness of a condition that countless people live with every day.

In my work in local government, in leadership and campaigning, I've faced prejudice and been patronised. Boards stacked with white middle-class men have stereotyped me based on race, sex and class, and attempted to sweep my opinions under the carpet. Comments I have received include: 'It must be hard for a Muslim woman to understand complex housing situations; do you learn everything by heart?' On one occasion, when I was Cabinet Member for Housing, I was asked to contribute to a parliamentary committee regarding the benefits of London hosting the Olympics in 2012. I sat outside the committee room with other lead members from Olympic host boroughs. I was the only woman and also the only person of colour. The other lead members were all white, middle-aged men. When the middle-aged white clerk came out to take people to the hearing, I was left behind.

I waited... and I waited.

Finally, a rather red-faced male clerk came to take me in. He had assumed I was a helper to one of the other Cabinet leads.

Ethnic minorities are frequently subjected to micro- and macroaggressions and while comments or behaviours are not always intentionally biased, they still have an impact.

But in spite of the slights, the knowledge and experience

I've gained through my work as a councillor and Cabinet Member for Housing has helped shape policies that empower people and improve their lives, and has also assisted the council and housing associations financially. I'm particularly proud of instigating Project 120, which helps build homes for people with complex abilities on new housing developments, so even before the spade hits ground, there is a personalised home set aside for a resident with profound needs. This helped saved money for the council and housing associations by preventing further work from being carried out if the home did not meet a disabled person's needs.

My decision to join the Liberal Democrats in August 2018 was based on my desire to remain in the European Union, and it was the only mainstream political party that had a clear stance on Europe even though it was at 4 per cent in the polls. I had begun to work with the local party members, who shared my values and strong sense of social justice, on local campaigns. My decision paved the way to the Lib Dems gaining their only Tower Hamlets councillor.

Obstacles and even defeat enable positive people to reflect and learn. In 2018, I stood again in the Tower Hamlets mayoral election, coming second to the Labour incumbent. Although I did not emerge as the victor, I see both results as victories, not only because I had the resilience to stand under immensely difficult circumstances, bearing criticism, abuse and false accusations, but also because it demonstrated that, although we might face higher hurdles, Muslim women can play a valuable part in public life.

A decade of life in the rough and tumble of both controversial and rewarding politics has taught me that life doesn't always run smoothly, but we can always learn from the setbacks. The best leaders are not afraid to admit their weaknesses, learn from them, accept failure and apologise for their mistakes. They seek to understand everyone's perspective so they can offer solutions that benefit everyone. They inspire others to reach their full potential, rather than focusing on maintaining their own position of power. And, most of all, they stand by people and create the conditions for positive change.

As I look over the years since I became an elected member, I recall interviews with other politicians who have lost elections, where it's often stated that one of the things they find most difficult to deal with is the sudden loss of attention. The phone stops ringing. People who wanted to be their best friend the day before the election suddenly aren't interested any more. Well, my phone didn't stop ringing when I went into opposition. I continued to be inundated with constituents wanting me to fight their corner. But there was a period where I felt like I was blacklisted. Despite no one ever having alleged that I had conducted myself improperly in office, some of my political opponents and parts of the media embarked on a heavy campaign of guilt by association. It wasn't really me that they had in their sights; it was the former mayor. But it was clear to me that they were content for my political career to become collateral damage.

They wanted me to disappear into obscurity. And if the

media continued to showcase my work as a political leader in my own right, it jarred with the narrative of the other sensationalist stories they were printing about the council supposedly being infiltrated by Islamists. So, they simply tried to airbrush me out of the political landscape. It was painful for me; I had gone into politics to make a contribution to society, and I wasn't done yet.

I refused to be collateral damage.

So I had to dust myself off and set about rebuilding my work from scratch. I went back to basics: working round the clock on cases raised by my constituents, mostly relating to the housing crisis, and to the work I had done with the media when I worked in the creative arts before I stood for election. And it was a long, hard slog. Media outlets weren't prepared to take me as they found me; they were suspicious that, somehow, I must be tainted by failures for which I had never been responsible. But, gradually, as I made my own way as an independent-minded campaigner for my local constituents, the mist cleared and the invitations to platforms and broadcasters' panel discussions began to return.

It is hard to describe the intensity of being systematically delegitimised and having your public profile unceremoniously snuffed out. That delegitimisation was also partly possible because of the way people saw Muslims in the post-9/11 era. Whereas other politicians seemed to have an entitlement complex, time and time again I was required to justify my very existence as an actor on the political stage.

I had to sing for my supper; to earn my right to participate in British politics. And for many that challenge would have been insurmountable, but it was not new to me. As a Muslim woman, from the beginning I had always been required to justify myself, and disassociate myself from people or organisations or ideologies I'd never heard of, in order to participate in politics. I would read one of my favourite poems, the enduring words of 'Still I Rise' by Maya Angelou; reach out to my brother and sisters, my husband, my children and my mother; and search within myself for strength, resilience and that ultimate belief that I could keep going.

I hope that those who stand on my shoulders are made to feel more welcome.

CHAPTER 12

WHITE PRIVILEGE AND MUSLIM WOMEN

On 28 August 1963, the Rev. Martin Luther King Jr delivered his iconic and much-quoted 'I Have a Dream' speech at the Lincoln Memorial in Washington DC. Although it is nearly six decades since he said, 'I have a dream that my four little children will one day live in a nation where they will not be judged by the colour of their skin but by the content of their character', our children are still being judged, first and foremost, by the colour of their skin and, in the case of Muslim girls, their attire.

As a child, every Saturday after lunch, my dad took me and my siblings down Rochester High Street to the library. Whether we were basking in the sunshine, battling the wind or wrapping up warm in the snow, we would walk down Rochester Vines, past the cathedral and Charles Dickens's house. As my father led his little brood, white people would often turn round to stare at us, and he would proudly look back at them.

In the 1980s, my colourful assortment of the jelly sandals and jelly bags that were in fashion were not exactly Dad's idea of common sense. He would always have an extra pair of socks in his pocket in case it rained and my feet got cold, and he insisted I put my books in a carrier bag inside my pink jelly bag. Explaining the fashion aspect to my parents was not a winning argument because common sense in protecting feet and books prevailed.

We would walk along the High Street, peeping into the antique shops while Dad popped into the British Gas shop to pay our bills. I would look through the windows of Tudor-built old-fashioned sweet shops selling cola cubes, pear drops and, my favourite, rhubarb and custard. Dad would buy a small bag of these and we would stick a sweet into each of our cheeks, stimulating a sugar rush. On the way to the library, we would ask when we could have a doughnut as we passed the different bakers and inhaled the intoxicating aroma of freshly baked doughnuts, cakes and rolls.

I remember the bakery where we bought our cream doughnuts and how we were treated by the white staff. Dad was not allowed to take all three of us into the bakery, so we would wait outside, holding hands. When we squashed our faces against the window, the assistant would scream at us to get off, so Dad would smile at us and gesticulate for us to move away, rolling his eyes as he did so. White mothers could take their little children in with them, who would ask directly for the cakes they wanted; we stood outside alone, pointing to the cakes through the window to indicate to Dad which ones we wanted. I know it hurt my dad when he saw this, but in a town where he needed a white foreman to go with him to apply for a mortgage because the bank didn't believe his employment status, even with his papers as proof, what could he do but just try his best to make things better?

I suppose the cream doughnuts came in handy.

I knew exactly what was happening, and I knew that the middle-class white customers could see it too, but they must have considered it acceptable for us to be treated like that.

At the library, Dad expected us to seek out and absorb all the books that we could find. Every weekend we returned home with stacks of books to devour before the following Saturday. Dad would always encourage me to read Charles Dickens; maybe he liked the notion of being British. But then my dad was so loyal to his country that years later he would not change from British Gas, British Electricity or BT, and insisted that my brother purchase a British Ford. Our house was full of British manufactured goods.

Beginning in the children's section of the library, I read all the Brothers Grimm fairy tales repeatedly, the Nancy Drew books and Enid Blyton's *Faraway Tree* series, taking me to different places and times. I read non-fiction books on diverse topics, from volcanoes to Queen Victoria. One day, I found a book about 'Moslems' and the people who followed the 'Mohammed religion'. I used to weave through shelves of books trying to find something, though not yet sure what it was. I was searching for something to fill a void that couldn't be filled by Nancy Drew.

I found many books by women writers, such as Judy Blume, author of *Are You There, God? It's Me, Margaret*. My mum found the book, read the word 'God', and asked me whether it was from the local parish.

Growing up in a home where we loved to learn and lose ourselves in poems and stories meant that we had to learn to navigate not just the books but the librarians. At the library, we faced the sinewy, bespectacled librarian and her sweaty, acne-faced assistant on reception. We would hand over our library cards and our books and she would take ages to check that they had been returned on time. In those days, it was all done through a library stamp, so we stood as she meticulously went over every book to check for damage while the customers behind us looked on impatiently. Following numerous visits, it occurred to me that the librarian took more time checking our books than she did those of white families. It would niggle at me, and I would flare my nostrils at her as her beady eyes, magnified by her goldfish-bowl glasses, scrutinised each book while her veiny hands flicked through the pages. To me and my siblings, 'The Librarian' was an ominous, shady figure.

When we eventually got past border control, The Librarian would send her chubby assistant to check on us by pretending that he was tidying shelves. He was always armed with his stamp gun and wipes. If we chuckled audibly while reading a book, we would hear an even louder 'SHHH!'

emanating from nearby, and we would giggle to ourselves, trying to avoid being in the firing line of the assistant's saliva.

Although he followed us around the library, we were not really perturbed by his presence. It was The Librarian who made me angry, which eventually resulted in me having an argument with her when I was thirteen. On one visit to the library, after we had chosen our books and presented them at the desk, The Librarian wanted to look in my little sister's bag, because she thought that maybe a book had been put in her bag accidentally without being checked out. I could tell the red-faced assistant had something do with it as he nervously began to work harder, checking books in and visibly sweating; doing everything he could to avoid looking at us. My little sister was aged six at the time and was becoming distressed.

I refused to let her check my sister's bag and told her that she would have to call the police if she wanted to do that. The Librarian was shocked. For so long, this white woman had used her position to undermine us in a place where she had authority that, when challenged, she did not know what to say. There were people watching this altercation; even the subtle sound of pages turning could no longer be heard, as people became more engaged with us than with the books they were reading.

I repeated again that she needed to call the police if she wanted to check my little sister's bag. By now, my sister was openly crying and shaking in fear, as we did not have our dad with us for protection. White families watched and we felt vulnerable. Suddenly, a frail-looking white woman who was seated in a corner stood up and came over to us. She put her arm around my sister and told the librarian that we children had done nothing wrong. Her name was Phyllis Mary Room, and she became our family friend.

The Librarian withdrew to her desk, but I could feel her venomous stare.

Phyllis took us out, walked us down the road and bought candyfloss for us. Every weekend we would meet her in the library. She met our parents, and we visited her home with our mother. In turn, she came to our house for tea. Phyllis had been a teacher and was very well off; a middle-class woman with lots of books and a dusty home who was delighted to have our exotic company. Phyllis touched my life because she gave me confidence and hope that I could challenge people knowing someone would look out for me.

For me, Phyllis was a white privileged woman stepping in to defend me against another woman who used her own white privilege against children.

In my early teens, I began taking my sisters through the High Street to the library without our dad, and on the way back, we would visit the bakery. I decided that my sisters would not be standing outside the bakery like I was made to do as a little girl. The first day I took my sisters inside, it was the same woman who had served us for years, and she motioned for me to take my sisters outside. I ignored her. I recognised the male assistant as the older brother of one of the girls with whom I went to school. He looked extremely embarrassed at what the woman was doing, so he decided to take my order before that of the three customers in front of me.

The female assistant began to shake her head, her frizzy red hair poking out under her cap, matching her angry flushed face.

'They need to be outside, you know; it's a small shop.'

For years, this woman had used her white privilege to treat me differently, so there was no way she was getting away with it this time. I was ready to give up the doughnuts.

I ignored her, and the young man carried on with the order.

'I won't say it again; I'll have to tell the manager.'

That is when I snapped. 'Tell the manager!'

I wanted to ask her where the sign was that said brown children had to be outside while white children could be inside with their parents.

In complete shock, her mouth dropped open to reveal a line of silver fillings glistening in the sun that streamed through the windows. The other customers, three big burly white men, turned around to look at me with my skinny legs in a blue and white C&A dress, freshly washed black hair and angry face, with two little girls in plaits and ribbons peeping from behind me.

I folded my arms across my chest, my heart pounding, and smiled defiantly at the other customers, while my sisters dug their fingers nervously into the back of my dress. The three men stared at me and I stared back, trying hard not look at one of the men's tattoos of a huge serpent.

Suddenly, they burst into laughter and one of them said, 'Go on, love; there's enough room here for the little ones. Go enjoy your doughnuts.'

As time went by and I continued to take my siblings into the bakery, they were eventually allowed to point to the cakes and doughnuts they wanted to purchase. I shall never forget how the young assistant and the three other customers took my side against the hostile white woman. That day I learned how important it was to stand up against injustice and discrimination and those who sustain it.

• • •

In the late 1970s, books by black and Asian writers were not provided in school, so I was unaware that they existed. I did not read works by Maya Angelou and Alice Walker until later in life, and they had a profound effect on me. Writer, poet and civil rights activist Maya Angelou proved that you can face prejudice, pain, misogyny and adversity yet manage it successfully and experience joy. Her autobiography, *I Know Why the Caged Bird Sings*, covers racism, segregation, displacement and resistance in a philosophical and sometimes humorous way. Alice Walker, an African American writer, poet and social activist, is best known for tackling themes of race and gender. She was also the first African American woman to win the Pulitzer Prize for Fiction but is probably most renowned for her novel *The Color Purple*, which addresses the oppression that black women have experienced throughout history in the rural south of the United States of America.

However, it was the story of the other Mrs Rochester, a Creole woman, in the 1966 book *Wide Sargasso Sea* by Jean Rhys that had the most impact on me. The novel covered Antoinette's traumatic youth, her attendance at a convent school with other young Creole girls, and later her marriage of bribery to Mr Rochester, who was desperate for money. Her husband renamed her 'Bertha', eventually taking her to England from Jamaica, only to imprison her in their home. The novel is a response to colonialism written from a female perspective. In Rhys's novel, Antoinette is caught in an oppressive society to which she does not fully belong – either in Europe or in Jamaica. *Wide Sargasso Sea* explores the power of relationships between men and women and encompasses feminist themes through its emphasis on female characters, non-conformity and embracing new ideas about women's standing in society. I could certainly identify with Antoinette's feeling of not belonging and of battling against preconceptions, not just as a teenager but today. That feeling of not quite fitting in and having to justify myself, to prove that I do belong; the way in which my mother felt displaced coming to Britain to join my father; our struggle to integrate with our neighbours and neighbourhood, school and British society in ways that white people don't experience.

As teenagers, it was easy for my white peers to find the shampoo they wanted, or the makeup that suited their skin. When they watched *Top of the Pops* or their favourite soaps, or were entertained at the theatre, they saw people of their race representing them.

During my teens, my parents were Allders shoppers, and I was fascinated by the makeup counter. There was nothing subtle about '80s makeup; the eyeshadows were vibrant, the foundation and eyeliner were thick, and the blushers were loud. Electric blue eyeshadow, fuchsia lips and cheeks that looked like a bad case of sunburn were all the rage.

One day, as I watched one of the makeup artists testing colours on a blonde woman, she looked over at me and smiled, her face caked with orange foundation, bright pink blusher and glossy lipstick. She called me over.

'Now darling, do you want me to dabble a bit of colour on you? Got lovely skin, you know; I could do so much.'

I climbed onto the high stool and proffered my face for Jean. While chewing gum and telling me about her boyfriend, she set to work squeezing out ginger foundation from a tube and, working from left to right, smoothed it across my face. I sat there nervously, wondering what the end result was going to look like. She then produced an eyeshadow palette of neon pinks and blues and proceeded to pull up the skin beneath my eyebrows to apply the shadow to my eyelids. It felt as though she was applying multiple layers, and my eyes watered each time she pressed on my eyeball. She applied blusher with a huge brush, sweeping it across my face from my ears to my nose, drew a line of bright blue eyeliner beneath my lower lashes and finished off with a generous dusting of powder.

Jean grinned with pride as she stood back to admire her handiwork. A couple of other customers walked past, looked at me and sniggered. What little excitement I had disappeared in that instant. I began to wonder why I had agreed to have this done to me in public.

Jean picked up a heart-shaped mirror and held it in front of my face. My heart sank when I saw the reflection of an orange face with fluorescent eyelids, unblended slashes of pink blusher and vivid pink lipstick.

'How do you like it?' asked Jean, clearly expecting a positive response.

I couldn't say what I really felt, so I smiled and said, 'Thanks, Jean. I look like you.'

By then, my parents had come down the lift and were looking for me. I called to them from where I sat. When they turned around to face me, Mum wailed, 'Ya Allah!' ('Oh God!') and dropped her bags. My dad looked terrified.

Although vibrant makeup in clashing colours was all the rage in the 1980s, and department store makeup artists have always been guilty of over-enthusiastic application, my experience in Allders was worsened by the lack of appropriate foundation and blusher shades for darker skin tones. Most makeup brands – especially the cheaper ones – didn't consider the various undertones of your skin; they simply created a graduated range from light to dark where the lightest made white women look like ghosts and the darkest shade looked like a bad fake tan. Fortunately, makeup choices for darker complexions have improved dramatically over the years.

• • •

When my eldest daughter, Zakia, was in Year 9, she went on a school trip to Kent with her classmates. The venue featured a set from Victorian literature, with model buildings and educational information about the history of the docks. There were tours, interactive shows, shops and a boat ride.

This tourist venue was not used to seeing 100 – mainly Bangladeshi – girls in mulberry-coloured shalwar kameez, some wearing headscarves and others not. There was another group of mainly white girls from a local school who were visiting on the same day.

Zakia's year group popped in and out of the souvenir shops, but the shopkeepers followed them around, shouted at them and accused them of attempting to steal. They were made to feel like criminals and had to endure the embarrassment of disgusted looks from the owners and other customers, including white schoolgirls who squealed with laughter.

Outside one of the shops, a white schoolgirl threw crisps and drinks at my daughter and her classmates, shouting, 'Dirty bunch of Pakis.'

Finally, one of Zakia's friends threw a punch at one of the

girls, and the shopkeepers came out asking for the teacher in charge. She looked angrily at her pupils.

When they returned to school, her year group were told to stand in line by the white teacher who had accompanied them; she had called for the headteacher to act as judge and jury of the incident.

However, Zakia's head of year, a Nigerian teacher, marched in and screamed, 'How dare you?' She defended the girls because she too had been a victim during the trip with the group.

Too often, innocent people of colour are automatically deemed guilty before they have even had a chance to prove otherwise. It took another woman of colour to step up and defend my daughter and her friends, while the white teachers were guilty of discrimination – conscious or not.

It is this bias that means that people of colour are still made to feel unwelcome, harassed, verbally assaulted and even subjected to violence. The appalling murder of George Floyd is just one example of this.

For many white people, the confidence that they're not personally guilty of active discrimination and hostility can feel comfortingly like 'job done'. But it's not enough to simply avoid being racist; it's also essential to acknowledge the ways in which some groups benefit from structural racism and the oppression of people of colour, even if it's inadvertent.

African American writer, teacher, sociologist and activist W. E. B. Du Bois transformed the way in which black citizens' lives were viewed in American society. Born in 1868,

Du Bois's first book, *The Suppression of the African Slave-Trade to the United States of America, 1638–1870*, became a standard in American education on slavery. In a later book, *Black Reconstruction in America*, Du Bois described whiteness as 'a sort of public and psychological wage' that provided lower-paid white workers with some measure of compensation that their black counterparts were denied.

> They were given public deference and titles of courtesy because they were white. They were admitted freely with all classes of white people to public functions, public parks, and the best schools. The police were drawn from their ranks, and the courts, dependent on their votes, treated them with such leniency as to encourage lawlessness. Their vote selected public officials, and while this had small effect upon the economic situation, it had great effect upon their personal treatment and the deference shown them.

Today we call it white privilege: the unearned, often unnoticed advantages that white or light-skinned people are still given by a society with a long history of discriminating against people of colour.

It has taken a long time for this concept to be recognised and accepted, even to a limited degree.

At school, I read Harper Lee's famous book *To Kill A Mockingbird*, the story of attorney Atticus Finch, who defends a black man, Tom Robinson, after he is wrongfully accused of the rape of a white girl from a poor background. While the book tackles racism, and suggests that standing up against oppression is everyone's responsibility, it also puts Atticus Finch on a pedestal: the central focus is not the black man suffering in a world rife with discrimination but the white man's moral virtue; it is the latter's humanity that is underscored throughout. When I was asked to talk about why I chose to read *To Kill A Mockingbird*, my white peers understood the book's message about the injustice of racial discrimination, but they found it hard to accept the idea that in romanticising Finch, the book itself both demonstrates and upholds white privilege.

I remember some of them rolled their eyes and I got angry, so I threw a rubber at one of the boys and the teacher shouted my name. That made me even angrier. Gritting my teeth, I explained:

It's all right for you all because you're white and I'm brown. When my dad goes to the bank, he's called after a white person even though he is in front of them. When I walk through a shop, the security guard doesn't hold the door for me, but he does for a white woman in front of me. And what about the fucking ice cream man who parks outside the school gates? We have to wait for ages to get an ice cream because he keeps serving white kids before us. Don't you get that your white skin has benefits?

I remember saying bitchily to one of the girls, 'But you know what? No matter how much you tan your skin, you won't get skin like ours.'

White privilege and racism are not the same things. Racism is direct discrimination, active prejudice based on a person's race, whereas white privilege is passive, a quiet acceptance of unearned benefits that are denied to others. The concept of white privilege, by definition, does not suggest that white people have never struggled, either individually or as a group, but that they have built-in advantages that are separate from any level of income or effort. White privilege means having greater access to resources and power than people of colour in the same situation do.

And yet even today, many white people can become defensive and sometimes angry when others suggest that they benefit – even passively and inadvertently – from living in a society that discriminates against people of colour.

When Emma Watson served as a United Nations Women Goodwill Ambassador, critics described her as a 'white feminist'. Watson had no idea why the qualifier 'white' had been attached to her feminism, and her instinctive response was to reject the label. It was only when she questioned herself more deeply that she understood the ways in which her advocacy of women's rights had focused on white women (and often middle-class white women), ignoring the unique challenges faced by women of colour. In an open letter to her feminist book club, Our Shared Shelf, she wrote:

When I heard myself being called a 'white feminist' I

didn't understand (I suppose I proved their case in point). What was the need to define me – or anyone else for that matter – as a feminist by race? What did this mean? Was I being called racist? Was the feminist movement more fractured than I had understood? I began… panicking.

It would have been more useful to spend the time asking myself questions like: What are the ways I have benefited from being white? In what ways do I support and uphold a system that is structurally racist? How do my race, class and gender affect my perspective? There seemed to be many types of feminists and feminism. But instead of seeing these differences as divisive, I could have asked whether defining them was actually empowering and bringing about better understanding. But I didn't know to ask these questions … As human beings, as friends, as family members, as partners, we all have blind spots; we need people that love us to call us out and then walk with us while we do the work.

As Watson suggests, the eagerness to build a movement and to find common cause has often led white feminists to focus on shared experiences – but to do so minimises or disregards the specific challenges faced by women of colour. Historically, it is white, middle-class women who have been the controlling voices of feminism (which may explain why they have focused so much on gender equality in prominent positions and overlooked the inequality at the bottom of the scale). White feminists have long viewed their task as a struggle against men – black, brown, white – without acknowledging the ways in which structural racism in society puts women of colour at an added disadvantage.

Institutional racism is defined as:

> the collective failure of an organisation to provide an appropriate and professional service to people because of their colour, culture or ethnic origin. It can be seen or detected in processes, attitudes and behaviour which amount to discrimination through unwitting prejudice, ignorance, thoughtlessness and racist stereotyping which disadvantage minority ethnic people.

Although women in general still face unconscious gender bias, particularly in the workplace, Islamophobia has a disproportionate effect on Muslim women. One study showed that religion has a greater impact on labour market outcomes than race or ethnicity, with Muslim women being the most disadvantaged compared to other religious minorities. Women from ethnic minorities tend to get paid less than white women with the same qualifications, facing what many researchers refer to as an 'ethnic penalty'.

Visibly Muslim women are also more likely to be targets of racism and violence. The Leveson Inquiry found that the press often reports in a way that damages the credibility of Muslims, but discussions in Parliament about banning the burqa also fuel existing discrimination. Without understanding how racism intersects with sexism to compound disadvantage for women of colour, we cannot have an honest conversation about women's rights.

Indeed, the fact that white feminists are given a greater media platform and more opportunity to shape the public debate is just one example of this structural power differential – and one that applies beyond discussions of feminism. As American actress Rowan Blanchard has pointed out on Instagram, 'We are so quick to applaud white women for commenting on race issues/discussions like #BlackLives-Matter, and #SayHerName, but when a Black girl comments on it – she is told she is overreacting or being angry.' And how many Muslim women are given the opportunity to write about how their lives are affected by prejudice, or about what feminism means to them? Are the views of Muslim feminists not deemed worthy of publication because of the false assumption that Muslim women are oppressed and therefore cannot be true feminists? In my experience, some people believe that Muslim women, especially those who wear the hijab, cannot possibly believe in women's rights as their attire and values in life are dictated by men. This may be true for a minority of women of all races and religions, including white women, but it is certainly not true for the majority of Muslim women in the UK.

Emma Watson should be applauded for her explicit acknowledgement that she has benefited from being white, and for openly asking herself the question: 'In what ways do I support and uphold a system that is structurally racist?' Those in a similar position of power have not always been so thoughtful. Lena Dunham, for instance, creator of the TV show *Girls*, which follows the lives of four young women in New York, was widely criticised for failing to cast a single person of colour as a main character in the first season of her TV show, despite one of the characters proclaiming herself 'the voice of my generation'. Even the supporting characters, critics noted, were predominantly white (a move jarringly at odds with the show's Brooklyn setting), while those characters of colour who did exist often sounded like stereotypes. In response, Dunham claimed that she wanted to avoid tokenism in casting and felt unqualified to write black characters: 'If I had one of the four girls, if, for example, she was African American, I feel like, not that the experience of an African American girl and a white girl are drastically different, but there has to be specificity to that experience [that] I wasn't able to speak to.' And yet this justification not only relies on presenting the show as the work of one person – avoiding awkward questions about why Dunham's writers' room was mostly white – but also offers no apology for failing to make space for people of colour in her fictional version of New York.

Dunham's brand of white feminism came in for more intense criticism in November 2017, when she implied that Aurora Perrineau, a woman of colour, was lying about having been raped at age seventeen by former *Girls* writer Murray Miller. Together with *Girls* showrunner Jenni Konner, Dunham released a statement saying, 'While our first instinct is to listen to every woman's story, our insider knowledge of Murray's situation makes us confident that sadly this accusation is one of the 3 percent of assault cases that are misreported every year.' By 'insider knowledge', they presumably meant that they had worked with Miller, not that they had first-hand information about the events Perrineau alleged. Dunham later admitted as much, apologising in an open letter to Perrineau:

> I didn't have the 'insider information' I claimed but rather blind faith in a story that kept slipping and changing and revealed itself to mean nothing at all. I wanted to feel my workplace and my world were safe, untouched by the outside world (a privilege in and of itself, the privilege of ignoring what hasn't hurt you) and I claimed that safety at cost to someone else, someone very special.

As Dunham later recognised, she had used her platform to hijack a conversation that didn't involve her, shouting down the experiences of a woman of colour – and she was enabled to do so by her position of white privilege.

Incidents like these shine a light on the relative power enjoyed by white feminists – but they also underline just how important it is to make space for women of colour to join the conversation. We saw in Chapter 4 how Amber Rudd's description of Diane Abbott as 'coloured' came, ironically enough, in the context of her broader point about black and ethnic minority women facing more abuse than their white counterparts. This was a woman who proudly declared

herself a staunch feminist, who showed at least some awareness of how different forms of discrimination intersect with
sexism – and yet the language she used was so shockingly
outdated that it overshadowed the point she was trying to
make. Rudd's comments were a stark reminder that even
when on the same feminist side, many educated people
struggle with basic vocabulary when talking about women
of colour – so how can we expect them to fight for our rights
alongside their own?

Even more worrying was that this was coming from a
senior government minister. When the interview aired, it
sparked a conversation between Liberal Democrat district
councillor for South Cambridgeshire Tumi Hawkins and
me. Tumi, also a woman of colour, agreed that while she
commended Ms Rudd for speaking up for black and minority ethnic women facing racism, she was shocked by
Rudd's use of the word 'coloured'. Tumi went on to note that
as the former Home Secretary who had inherited and perpetuated Theresa May's 'hostile environment' policy, which
resulted in the Windrush scandal, Rudd had represented an
enormous degree of institutional power over the lives of the
UK's minority ethnic citizens. Her lack of awareness therefore appeared to symbolise a more profound institutional
ignorance, illustrating the extent to which non-whites are
regarded as 'other' even by their own government.

For those not already familiar with it, the hostile environment policy was developed to discourage people from
coming to the UK, to prevent foreigners from overstaying

and to stop irregular migrants being able to access the same essential services as British citizens – work, housing, healthcare, bank accounts and so on. The unintended consequence, however, was serious discrimination against ethnic minority groups, with thousands of long-term, lawful residents being wrongly classified as illegal immigrants, many of them losing their jobs, homes and health.

The Windrush generation were those who arrived in the UK from the Caribbean between 1948 and 1973 to take up vital jobs in the NHS and other sectors affected by the post-war labour shortage. At the time, the Caribbean was part of the British Commonwealth, so these citizens were automatically regarded as British subjects who were free to live and work in the UK indefinitely – and so they did, building their lives here, raising their children, contributing to public services, making up part of the fabric of British society. After the hostile environment policy was instituted, it emerged that many of those from the Windrush generation lacked documentation proving their right to remain in the UK. Many had arrived as children on their parents' passports and had never applied for their own adult passport as they had no desire to leave their home country. In 2018, it emerged that the Home Office had destroyed thousands of landing cards and other records that proved Windrush citizens' right to live and work in the UK – despite having been warned that this would make it difficult or impossible for lawful immigrants to prove their legal status. The Home Office has admitted that at least 164 people have been wrongly detained or deported; at least eleven of those died without having received compensation.

This is why intersectionality is so important. How can we expect our government to act in the best interests of the communities they purport to represent if they don't understand them, if they see them as 'other', if they fail to recognise and address institutional discrimination? Much emphasis has – rightly – been placed on improving representation of women in government. But all of that counts for very little if the women elected to govern all come from the same narrow section of society and don't appreciate how profoundly their experiences have been shaped by the privileges they've been given. To achieve real progress in gender equality, we need to acknowledge all elements of social discrimination, including both gender and race, but also class, sexual orientation, age, religion and disability and understand how they intersect. It's easy for politicians to pay lip service to this issue, but to truly understand and empathise with struggles that have never affected them personally, they need to engage with other communities and create space for them to be part of the conversation. Feminism needs to take an intersectional stance in order to make a real difference, and we all need to acknowledge the privilege we're afforded, whether by our race, our religion or our class, if we're to come together to make real change, ensuring that all women benefit from women's rights.

CHAPTER 13

TOGETHER IN OUR STRUGGLES

It is 130 years since the London matchgirls' strike, instigated by women and teenage girls working at the Bryant and May factory in Bow in protest over their poor working conditions. Not only were they forced to work fourteen-hour days for very low wages, but their exposure to white phosphorus caused serious health conditions. 'Phossy jaw' induced toothache and flu-like symptoms, then tooth loss, abscesses and swelling of the gums, and finally necrosis of the jaw. If a Bryant and May worker reported toothache, they were ordered to have the teeth removed immediately, on pain of sacking. Three previous strikes had failed, but when the whole factory downed tools in July 1888, reforms were finally implemented.

While phossy jaw may be unheard of today, many of the problems confronting workers in the Victorian East End still resonate. Poverty, illiteracy, poor health, political repression and patriarchy still affect vast numbers of women in Britain and globally – Muslim women included. The story of the modern matchgirl is still about poverty, inequality and vastly unjust power dynamics. But it is also one of women working together to challenge those dynamics, carving out space for themselves and each other in a society that often seems content to ignore their suffering.

The first time I helped a woman flee domestic violence was in December 1993. It was cold and snowy that evening when I received a call from Samina, the project worker at Tower Hamlets Homeless Families Campaign, about the woman we were supporting. Samina intuitively felt that we should visit the woman immediately because she had tried calling her but the line was dead. In those days there were no mobile phones.

I dragged on my warmest coat and out we went. We knocked and stood on the doorstep, the snow falling around us. We could hear a toddler inside, but it was a good ten minutes of consistent knocking before the door opened. The woman we had come to see had a bloody face and was in shock. All she said was, 'Take me before he comes.'

Samina and I ran into the house. There was a newborn baby and three-year-old crying her eyes out. We wrapped the children in warm clothes and searched for the woman's documents. Preparing her to leave was the most difficult thing. She was terrified, almost immobile. We knew if we didn't hurry, the man would return and the whole neighbourhood would wake up.

Finally, we left the house. Samina had the toddler; I

carried the baby and their bags and together we encouraged the woman along the icy street. She had not been able to find a coat and, as she ran, her breast milk started to leak through her clothes. I covered her with my cashmere shawl. We turned the corner and never in my life had I been so happy to see the yellow light above a black cab. We waved it down and the driver took us straight to the refuge, to a safety that had become a distant memory as she endured nightly beatings accompanied by the cries of her frightened children.

In my surgeries, I speak to an endless stream of women living in refuges, terrified at the prospect of rebuilding their lives after a brief respite in a haven of safety. However, I also speak to women who are still living in their homes, either trying to escape abusive relationships or those who have left but are afraid of being stalked and attacked by ex-partners.

Single mothers have traditionally been targeted for vilification by politicians and the media, who have frequently portrayed them as feckless consumers of welfare. As recently as the '90s, it was routine for Conservative MPs to claim that women deliberately got pregnant to gain access to benefits, and we're governed today by a Prime Minister who as a *Spectator* columnist blamed single mothers for 'producing a generation of ill-raised, ignorant, aggressive and illegitimate children' – a stark irony coming from a man who refuses to confirm how many children he has fathered. However, the stigma faced by Muslim women in a tight-knit community is even more challenging, as the weight of family and community disapproval fuels an intense pressure to avoid separation or divorce. As a result, many of those trapped in abusive relationships feel isolated and are suffering in silence. Muslim women are affected by domestic abuse, sexual assault and rape as much as any other women, but are they receiving the attention and help that they need? Have we failed in looking after Muslim girls and women?

These problems are only worsened by the marginalisation of Muslim women in British society. For so many women of all faiths and none, there are already daunting obstacles to seeking help, such as not having the opportunity to make contact with support services without the knowledge of their abuser – and the arrival of the Covid-19 pandemic and 'stay at home' directive created the ideal environment for abusers to isolate, abuse and control their victims. When we add to that the extra barriers faced by Muslim women, who routinely face prejudice from others, it should be no surprise that many feel utterly isolated from possible sources of support.

Of course, attacks on multiculturalism are not new: whether you consider the infamous 'Rivers of Blood' speech made by Enoch Powell, or Margaret Thatcher and her notorious comments about Britain being 'swamped by people of a different culture' before she won the 1979 general election, politicians have all too frequently stirred up racial discrimination for their short-term electoral advantage. So it was no surprise to me when David Cameron used an early speech as Prime Minister to blame multiculturalism for radicalisation and terrorism. At a security conference in Munich in February 2011, Mr Cameron claimed that 'state multiculturalism' had failed, 'weakening our collective identity' and encouraging 'different cultures to live separate lives, apart from each other and apart from the mainstream'. With spectacularly ill-judged timing – or perhaps simply indifference to how his words would affect British Muslims – he made these comments on the same day the UK saw one of its largest ever anti-Islam rallies, with 3,000 English Defence League supporters marching through Luton chanting Islamophobic slogans.

Critics of multiculturalism frequently point to mosques as a symbol of Muslims' separatism from British society, suggesting, indirectly or otherwise, that they are a breeding ground for extremism. However, what these critics fail to understand is that building a mosque, temple, synagogue or faith-based community centre is not a sign of wanting to be separate but a sign of saying 'we belong here', that Britain is our home and our community, and it is where we want to put down roots. They can also be a powerful focus for mutual aid.

The first mosque in England was founded in 1889 in a mid-terrace house in Liverpool by an English solicitor, William Henry Quilliam, who had converted to Islam two years earlier, taking the name Abdullah. Humayun Ansari, professor of the history of Islam at the Royal Holloway University of London, said that the life Quilliam saw in Morocco appealed to him: 'He felt that people lived simple – they lived, in his view, quite moral lives and there was an environment of solidarity, depending very little on whether they were wealthy or poor. That was something that was of immense significance for him.' Over the years, the mosque, known as the Liverpool Muslim Institute, grew to include a museum, a science laboratory, a library, schools and an orphanage.

When I was a pre-schooler, local Muslims came to our tiny house in Chatham, Kent, for Friday prayers until my father, Mohammed Abdul Quadir, helped found the first mosque in the town in an end-of-terrace house at the bottom of the hill in the early 1980s. Local people knew my dad and trusted him. Older men, both Muslims and non-Muslims, used to drop in for a chat, not about religion or philosophy but about their grandchildren, the latest episode of *Only Fools and Horses* and all the everyday chit-chat that greases the wheels of civil society. One of my father's friends was a non-Muslim man, Bert, who worked at British Gas; they had become friends when Bert first came to fix our boiler, but it was a relationship that lasted a lifetime. Long gone were the days when my father faced daily abuse; not bigotry exactly, but the casual slurs also aimed at the Irish, or someone supporting a different football team – the typical working-class knockabout humour that was prevalent forty years ago but not necessarily accepted now.

Our local mosque had a positive impact on the local community by undertaking charitable work, organising aid for the needy and vulnerable and helping to transform residents' lives. In their 'Mosques in Communities' project, which set out to understand the role of mosques in relation to their local communities, the Mosques and Imams National Advisory Board said that if faith-based centres 'rise to the challenge of becoming community hubs', transforming their buildings into venues where people can socialise and organise activities and projects for the benefit of the local community, 'they can bring about real change', promoting better relations between neighbours, bringing local people together, encouraging volunteering and civic responsibility, and fostering democracy.

These community hubs and their involvement in bringing about change are particularly relevant in tackling problems and prejudice relating to women. Traditionally, mosques have been male-dominated establishments, but today women have much greater involvement. The Women in Mosques Development Programme was launched in 2018–19 to offer bespoke training sessions across the UK to high-potential upcoming female leaders, to support them in becoming trustees, committee members and project officers of their local mosques. In January 2021, Zara Mohammed was the first woman to be elected as the Secretary General of the Muslim Council of Britain. She said that her vision is to 'continue to build a truly inclusive, diverse and representative body; one which is driven by the needs of British Muslims for the common good'. Another influential Muslim woman is Akeela Ahmed MBE, an equalities campaigner specialising in youth and gender issues. She is the founder of She Speaks We Hear, an online platform that brings women together to share their experiences and tell their stories without being 'hijacked by others for their own political or ideological aims'. There are many more Muslim women who are working at a local level to elicit change, and hopefully this will translate into greater representation of Muslim women in national leadership roles.

Indeed, Muslim women have far more agency than the stereotypes suggest and have been actively effecting change in a variety of ways. In 2003, with the support of the Women's National Commission, a group of women came together to offer independent advice to the government on issues relating to Muslim women and public policy. Initially named Muslim Women's Network, the group changed its name to Muslim Women's Network UK after it was established as a community interest company in 2008. Its aim is to help to challenge attitudes and stereotypes, inform policy and practice, inform awareness campaign work and initiate open conversations about topics that are frequently ignored.

During the A-level results fiasco of 2020, women from different backgrounds came together to challenge the government on the system used to award grades following the cancellation of exams due to coronavirus. The original algorithm took into account not only each pupil's estimated grade, as assessed by their teacher, and their class ranking, but also their school's performance in each subject over the previous three years. The idea was to ensure that the schools' grades were consistent with those in the past, avoiding grade inflation. The result was that pupils from under-performing schools were unfairly penalised. In the UK overall, nearly 40 per cent of the grades were lower than teachers' assessments – and students from lower socioeconomic backgrounds and black, Asian and ethnic minority communities were disproportionately marked down, while those from small independent schools benefited the most, compounding their existing advantage over their peers. This prompted the Equality and Human Rights Commission to intervene, with its CEO, Rebecca Hilsenrath, saying that Ofqual must remove bias. Women from different backgrounds came together to challenge the government on this issue; Anjum Peerbacos, a teacher, writer and radio commentator, summed up the mood for many when she tweeted: 'We cannot accept yet another disadvantage for our children. As a senior teacher, a mother and being from a minority who are disadvantaged already, I know it is imperative that this injustice is reversed.'

But although the government eventually performed a U-turn, belatedly agreeing to drop the systematically unfair algorithm, the episode is just one example of how coronavirus has worsened existing structural inequalities that discriminate against people from black, Asian and ethnic minority communities. In order to address the significant impact of Covid-19 on individuals and society as a whole, and to continue to tackle structural racism and inequality, we need fair representation of Muslim women in leadership positions nationwide. The pandemic has forced us all to approach many things in a different way; in making sweeping changes, it's essential we ensure that our 'new normal'

includes driving out all forms of discrimination and ensuring that everyone is treated equally and given an opportunity to have their voices heard, regardless of race, gender,
religion, disability or sexual orientation.

Muslim women are often accused of not integrating, but
it is not so much a question of not wanting to integrate as
of facing difficulties integrating – and, often, being equally
criticised for integrating successfully. Many Muslim women
have faced challenges through pre-judgement, particularly those wearing the hijab, because of the false stereotype
that insists Islam is incompatible with gender equality and
female empowerment. There have been many stories in the
media of Muslim women removing their hijabs and even
changing their names to sound more 'English' in order to
secure employment or avoid confrontation in the workplace.
But many also face discrimination from within the Muslim
community, whether they opt to disguise their faith or not.
If we could move past discrimination instead of investing
our energy into disproving the stereotypes, or even hiding
our true identities in order to be accepted, then we Muslim
women have the potential to contribute so much more.

It may seem odd, but it is not just non-Muslims who have
been accused of Islamophobia but Muslims themselves.
As a Policy Exchange report notes, the term 'Islamophobia' has sometimes been used 'as a "heckler's veto" to shut
down alternative points of view ... thereby engaging in the
ultimate form of gatekeeper politics'. I've seen this dynam-
ic at work first hand. I was introduced to Dr Adnan Sharif

during the peak of the first Covid-19 lockdown, when I worked with many people across London and the country so that we could support vulnerable communities through the vicious onslaught of loss, grief and immense pressure wrought by the pandemic. Adnan is a consultant transplant nephrologist at a hospital in Birmingham, where one of the highest numbers of deaths have occurred. In April 2020, he was quoted in a *Sunday Times* article about his concerns in preparing for Ramadan, which the paper headlined 'Expert fears a spike in UK coronavirus cases if communities gather for Ramadan', and I later quoted the article on Twitter.

I was met with a diatribe of angry tweets from some Muslims, including one calling me an Islamophobe. Many people took exception to the title of the article, because they felt it implied that some Muslims might flout the lockdown rules. The article sparked debate and controversy across all media outlets and even a research project at Lancaster University. However, it is not Islamophobic to be worried that some people might break the lockdown rules during Ramadan; it is a perfectly reasonable concern. While we hoped that most Muslims would adhere to social distancing, we knew that not all would – and not all did. A friend of mine who lives next door to Muslim neighbours said that they had not observed social distancing since the beginning of lockdown:

Not only had they continued to entertain large groups of people from different families, but they celebrated Ramadan and Eid with a large party in their house. There were a lot of small children present, and this family has three young children, including a newborn baby. Whilst I re-alise that most Muslims are law-abiding, as with all races and religions, there are some who are not.

Of course, the same applies to white communities. To take just one of many high-profile examples, the Prime Minis-ter's top adviser, Dominic Cummings, broke the lockdown rules multiple times in a series of flawed judgements, and then compounded the offence by claiming to the nation that he had taken a trip to Durham beauty spot Barnard Castle on Easter Sunday 2020 (which also happened to be his wife's birthday) in order to test his eyesight. And just look at the footage from Bournemouth beach during the spells of hot sunny weather and see the large numbers of white people failing to listen to social distancing advice, selfishly putting themselves, their families and other people at risk. On 25 June 2020, these mass gatherings led Bournemouth, Christchurch and Poole Council to declare a major incident.

When dealing with the public health crisis caused by coro-navirus, there is a genuine concern about any occasion that might prompt people to gather in large groups, and how that might affect the overall coronavirus case rate – but, im-portantly, Dr Sharif was also quite rightly pointing out that when minority ethnic communities are disproportionately affected by Covid-19, it is important for people from these communities to take extra precautions to protect themselves and their families. He said that between 35 and 40 per cent of his hospital's admissions were patients from minority ethnic backgrounds, adding, 'For us, Ramadan is a big concern. Anything that leads to more social interaction is a big worry and Ramadan is by its very nature a community thing.'

Nonetheless, some suggested that Dr Adnan had been careless and irresponsible in giving his opinion. One person wrote: 'You are both in the frontline as visible Muslims; a woman in hijab working in politics and a very obviously Muslim man in the medical field. You're supposed to be the intelligent, responsible ones, lest you forgot.' Not everyone agreed; it was heartening to read tweets in support of us too. One person replied, 'Are you blaming them for doing their civic duty? ... Please fellow Muslims don't join the list of people from other communities who took a blasé attitude and chanced it just because of annual traditions.'

Of course, there is a legitimate point to be made that in speaking out to try to prevent excess deaths in minority ethnic communities, we must be mindful of the risk of feeding ingrained prejudice. As the World Health Organization's Covid-19 guidance states, 'words matter' and certain words could 'fuel stigmatised attitudes', provoking social stigma against people of certain ethnic backgrounds. We must all take this guidance seriously to avoid perpetuating negative racial stereotypes, creating fear and even dehumanising people who have the disease.

But while it's possible to have differences of opinion about public health policy, and about the possibility of public health concerns fuelling anti-Muslim sentiment in the UK if not carefully couched, what alarmed me was the way some people who disagreed with us immediately leapt to accuse us of Islamophobia. As the Policy Exchange report points out, the Islamophobe label is sometimes used to imply that certain Muslims 'sit outside the boundaries of the Islamic community. In short, the levelling of allegations of Islamophobia against Muslims represents an insidious, implicit form of takfir (excommunication), the process that in the hands of radicals might legitimate the targeting of ex-Muslims, and even reformist Muslims, with violence.'

It often seems as though the moment Muslims add our voice to topical issues, we are criticised by all sides, and yet we are excluded from many other discussions that affect the nation as a whole. The climate change debate, for example, has largely been dominated by middle-class voices, and yet people of colour are disproportionately affected by air pollution. According to a recent University of California study, black families who are segregated in inner cities are nearly twice as likely to die as other residents during a heatwave, not least of contaminated air.

In May 2020, the BBC reported that 'climate activism fails to represent BAME communities', suggesting that people of colour joining protests often fear violence and hostility from the police. The mother of nine-year-old Ella Kissi-Debrah, whose fatal asthma attack in 2013 was found to have been partly caused by illegal levels of pollution, pointed out that people from minority ethnic backgrounds are often invisible in the climate protest. We need to find ways of breaking down the barriers and encouraging more people of colour to become involved in climate change campaigns.

It is often those same minority ethnic communities who are vastly affected who do not have the information they need on climate change, and we need to do a lot more in reaching out to them – though I do not like it when we talk about educating people; we should really be talking about empowering people. Rather than condescending to them, we need to talk about empowering minority ethnic communities to understand more about how climate change affects them and what steps they can take on a personal level to make beneficial changes. There are so many easy ways to do this, and I remember one particular campaign during the month of Ramadan about stopping people from smoking. These are the things that matter.

Representative leadership can make a real difference, but it's often an uphill battle. In July 2019, two weeks before a Tower Hamlets council meeting, I emailed the (white female) councillor who held the brief for climate change, drawing her attention to the substantial evidence that the climate change debate is not as inclusive as it should be and proposing an amendment to a motion due to be debated at the forthcoming meeting. The council, I proposed, could resolve to deliver a programme of community climate change engagement to build awareness and support, and empower minority ethnic groups to engage with the projects around climate change. We could, for instance, build a targeted awareness message by drawing on the inter-faith calendar, perhaps linking fasting during Ramadan to the concept of reducing food waste, and encouraging parents to recycle by reaching out through school engagement projects. I wrote that I would still support the motion even if my amendment wasn't accepted but noted that from my experience of working with such communities, we need to improve the way in which the climate change debate engages with them.

The councillor did not respond at all.

At the full council meeting, however, she proposed an updated version of her motion. In the motion were the exact words that I included in my email request, disingenuously made to look like her own amendment. Before I made my speech I pointed this out, but she still did not acknowledge it. For me, this is white privilege.

This is not just about who gets credit for their work, although many people will be uncomfortable with a white woman presenting a Muslim woman's ideas on minority inclusion as her own, myself included. It matters because acknowledging the contribution made by people from minority backgrounds is crucial to engaging with those communities and improving integration. It also matters because words, however well meaning, have to be backed up by effective action. Too often, positive noises about diversity and inclusion are used as a substitute for tangible change by people with no real stake in the outcome.

Although it was a white female councillor who proposed the motion, it was a black woman who spoke on the climate change amendment I had suggested. There was a failure from the proposer of the motion to mention that it was a woman of colour who had initiated the idea. It isn't a case of blowing one's own trumpet, but one of acknowledging the contribution made by women of all ethnicities so that they will be judged by their performance rather than by their race or colour.

Let's compare the response from that white female Labour councillor to that of Amy Whitelock Gibbs, another white female former Labour councillor. Going back to August 2017, there was a furore about a foster care case in Tower Hamlets, with a Muslim foster care family demonised for allegedly forcing a non-Muslim child in their care to adopt Muslim values. A series of articles in *The Times* gave a deeply one-sided account of the situation, suggesting that a 'white Christian child' had been 'forced into Muslim foster care' by the council, only to be ordered by a judge to remove the child and place her instead with her grandmother. In fact, the council had requested the girl be placed with her grandmother, who was herself from a Muslim background. The foster carers involved were left distraught at the media reporting of the case, and Tower Hamlets Council received abusive phone calls.

At the time, I wrote an article for *The Independent* on the topic, stating that a safe environment is better than a familiar one. The following month, I emailed Amy, the then Cabinet Member for Children's Services, proposing an amendment to her motion on foster care ahead of the council meeting later that evening. My proposed amendment clarified that the council regarded the media's reporting as Islamophobic and set out the council's intention to report the newspapers involved to IPSO. I pointed out that the story had done huge damage to efforts to recruit foster carers from diverse backgrounds in the very aim of promoting cultural matches, and that the Muslim community at large had been heavily bruised by the reporting, as is so often the case, adding, 'It is therefore vital that we demonstrate action to match our words that incidents of this kind are unacceptable.'

Amy responded the same day, saying she was minded to accept the amendment pending the agreement of others in the group and thanking me for a constructive approach to the issue. At the meeting, Amy brought her motion, creating space for me to introduce the amendment, which was duly accepted. The council subsequently received an apology from *The Times* after IPSO upheld the complaint, ruling that the original article had distorted the issue and failed to take care over accuracy.

To me, the difference between these two responses was enormous. I was the only female opposition councillor, not least a Muslim one in a hijab. In the climate change case, the councillor may have had good intentions in adopting my language for her motion, but given her failure to respond to me, her use of my words without any acknowledgement felt like an illustration of white female power not wishing to give credit to a hijab-wearing Muslim woman's views. It made me think about how white middle-class women who call themselves feminists often fail to recognise that this privilege can actually be their greatest barrier to bringing about change. There is an unconscious bias harboured by those in leadership roles, predominantly focusing on issues that affect white people and contributing to what has been termed 'toxic feminism'.

In contrast, Amy Whitelock Gibbs's swift and positive response, welcoming the proposal while stating the need for the group to agree the amendments, was that of a white woman who had listened and accepted that a cross-party working would bring change; and it did. I remember that meeting clearly, because Councillor Whitelock Gibbs smiled at me and nodded when she said the Labour group would accept the amendment. It is this kind of collaborative politics that helps to bring about positive change.

Intersectionality is absolutely vital. Equality and discrimination are not just white issues; they affect women of all races, and white feminists need to listen to experiences that are not their own if we are to bring about meaningful societal change and achieve true equality.

Until the Race Relations Act was first passed in November 1965, racial discrimination was not regarded as a crime. Even after the Race Relations Act, when my father tried to negotiate his first mortgage with a building society, his evidence that he met the requirements was questioned. My father produced every item the building society required, from receipts to show he had paid his utility bills to payslips showing overtime hours to references from his previous landlords. He was one of the few men of colour attempting to negotiate his mortgage at the building society. It was only when his foreman, Bob, insisted that he would accompany him to the next meeting that the mortgage was agreed. Bob became a family friend for years; it is people like him who have helped immigrant communities to integrate when the barriers thrown up by structural racism have been difficult and glacially slow to break down.

Years later, when I recounted this incident to my friend Roderick Lynch, he related an incident where he wanted to purchase a property but the white woman selling it had increased the asking price when he went to view it. When his white friend went to view the same property, the woman kept the price as it was. Roderick's ancestors were enslaved people from the Caribbean paradise island of Saint Lucia and in our conversations about race and racism he often says, 'Fighting racism is not for the swift but for those who can endure it.'

Although we have come a long way since then, Britain still faces a crisis around racial injustice, and we desperately need a new discourse on race and faith politics. These are controversial and sensitive topics that many people have been afraid to confront. However, as the Black Lives Matter campaign demonstrates, marginalised people now feel empowered to tackle these issues and fight for their rights. Although a lot has changed, especially with regard to diversity and inclusion in the workplace, and equal representation on TV, all of us have a responsibility not only to reject prejudice, religious intolerance and damaging stereotypes but to ensure we make space in the conversation for those whose voices have long been silenced. Within the feminist movement there is the potential for women of all races and faiths to contribute, working together to challenge those unjust power dynamics that continue to hold us back – but it requires us all to be mindful of those whose voices aren't being heard.

CHAPTER 14

MY VEIL AND HOPE

Whether we are Muslim or non-Muslim, veiled or un-veiled, women face barriers of prejudice, stereotypes and discrimination, which have often been further entrenched by the media.

Of course, the portrayal of women in the media has certainly improved since the 1970s, though admittedly it began from a low bar. In the 1980s, we saw the emergence of TV shows featuring marginalised groups of women, such as *The Golden Girls* and *Roseanne*. At the same time, women were beginning to be depicted in roles that had previously been male-dominated, such as police officers in crime dramas and powerful women in soap operas such as *Dynasty* and *Dallas*. These roles still had elements of sexism – the woman's role was often about winning over a man – but they represented an important step forward. In the 1990s, there was a positive shift towards female heroes holding their own, such as *Xena:*

Warrior Princess, and strong, competent, economically stable single women in shows such as *Sex and the City*.

In real life, meanwhile, change was also afoot, albeit gradually. In 1997, 120 female MPs entered Parliament following Labour's election victory. Although this doubled the number of women in in the Commons, it still meant that women accounted for less than one in five MPs. Even today, only 220 of our 650 MPs are women – little more than the 30 per cent floor set by the United Nations as the critical mass required to ensure that the representation of women is normalised and will continue. The Commons is still overwhelmingly populated by white men, with 402 taking their seats in the 2019 election.

Actress Geena Davis, who has long fought for gender equality, has said that when asked to picture a CEO, President, Hollywood director, top scientist, leading surgeon and so on – and in the UK we could safely add MP to that list – most people will picture a white man. The situation is not helped, she believes, by the fact that the media, entertainment and advertising industries continue to cement those mental images with their output, something that she is attempting to change with her non-profit organisation, the Geena Davis Institute on Gender in Media, and her #StrengthHasNoGender campaign.

Muslim women have had an even harder battle to dispel the myths and misrepresentations perpetuated by the media – not helped by the fact that these stereotypes extend even into the classroom, taking root from a young age. The history lessons we were taught as children shaped some of my peers' views of Muslim women. Our teachers taught us how much India benefited from having the British Raj, informing us that ayahs (nannies) were not just servants but oppressed women, who often had veils on their heads. Aside from that, history lessons rarely covered Islam, and when it did become part of religious education in schools in more recent years, some parents pulled their children out of the lessons because they didn't want them learning about any faith other than Christianity. Sadly, fundamentalism exists in all religions, and it is this attitude that promotes division and discourages our future generations from learning to live with others from different backgrounds.

Prior to colonial exploration, there was little contact in the Western world with veiled Muslim women. The perceptions of Muslim women that existed prior to the seventeenth century were based purely on tales of male travellers and inaccurate translations of Arabic texts. It was only in the eighteenth century that colonial expansion created a Western view of women in Islam. During the Victorian era, Muslim women and the idea of a harem were often the focus of men's erotic fantasies, particularly the idea of removing a woman's veil and uncovering the woman's body. At the same time, Orientalist paintings portrayed naked or scantily clad women in harems, which some interpreted as wanting to be rescued from cruel Eastern men by Western men. However, Western men were prohibited from entering harems where unveiled women could be viewed. Therefore, removing the veil was the ultimate form of colonisation. These tropes trickled down through the familiar narratives of Arabian Nights, Sinbad the Sailor and Aladdin. Most of these stories that our teachers read us at school depicted seductive, veiled women as victims who needed saving – although the queen in Arabian Nights was not a vulnerable woman but a courageous and intelligent one, with a gift for poetry and storytelling that saved her life and that of her sister.

Some of the boys in my class winked at me when the images of seductive veiled women came up. One day in the dinner hall as we finished the Lord's Prayer, a couple of the boys sat with me at my table and kept smiling at me. As they gobbled down sausages and mash, one of them looked up and said, 'Rabina, or should I say Ribena?', knowing that this would set me off.

'What?!' I seethed, gritting my teeth and clenching my fork.

'You know that scarf and that skirt on that woman in the picture we saw in class. Do you wear that at home?'

'What do you mean?' I asked, glaring at him.

'You know – like this.'

He stopped eating, stood up and moved his hips around as he tried to do a belly dance; everyone sniggered.

I got up and helped him finish his mash by shoving it in his face.

As I think about this now, it seems extraordinary how Muslim women have gone from pin-ups to victims in need of liberation to terrorists. How many labels can we possibly have?

When I was young, we were defined less by our religion than by our colour. I recall the first parents' evening I attended with my mother and my siblings at my Church of England school in Rochester. The teacher stared at us all and said to me, 'You look a bit darker than your sister, and you look a bit fairer than your other sister, and your mother looks really fair. Your brother looks the darkest.' I thought, *I'm here to talk about my studies, not my shade or colour*, but the teacher kept going until I wanted to say, 'Well, my mum hasn't been with the milkman, for sure.'

Communities were often described as British-Bangladeshis or British-Pakistanis – up until the Twin Towers attacks. Post-9/11, these communities increasingly found themselves referred to as Muslims, despite the fact that – as with all religions – there are practising and non-practising Muslims among us. Along with this came the view that the veil was a symbol of extremism.

Twenty years later, the wearing of the veil is still associated with extremism, gender inequality and oppression – and, ironically, it's not uncommon for those who believe Muslim women are oppressed to subject them to harassment and mistreatment. There are countless examples of women facing persecution for following their faith. In 2017, for example, a security guard at a McDonald's restaurant in London told a Muslim woman to remove her headscarf and blocked her from getting to the tills to order her food. She filmed the incident and the employee was subsequently suspended.

Like so many women across the world, I welcomed Hillary Clinton's declaration that 'women's rights are human rights'. For Muslim women worldwide, this should apply whether they wear the hijab or not, in the same way that women from diverse cultures and religions choose to adorn their bodies in the attire of their choice, or decorate themselves with piercings, tattoos and extreme hair colours. (Believe it or not, even Muslim women have pink, green, purple or blue hair beneath their hijabs!)

There are, however, vociferous Muslim women who oppose full-face veiling, particularly in the West, where they enjoy freedom of opinion and speech. Fadela Amara, a French Muslim politician and feminist, wrote that it 'is a mistake to see the veil as only a religious issue ... It is first of all a tool of oppression, alienation, discrimination, and an instrument of men's power over women. It is not an accident that men do not wear the veil.'

There are indeed women around the world who are forced to wear the full veil. Soutiam Goodarzi, for example, lived in Iran until the age of nine, when she moved to Britain, and was first made to wear the hijab when she was six. She wore it out of fear of encountering the 'modesty' police, who patrolled the streets in search of women not wearing a hijab. Schoolgirls were also subjected to other indignities, such as personal checks of their hair, and of their ears, wrists and chests for jewellery. In 2019, Goodarzi wrote an article for

The Spectator entitled 'There's nothing liberating about being forced to wear a hijab'. But of course, the clue is there in the headline – there's nothing liberating about being forced into wearing anything, whether it's a hijab or high heels, a jilbab or a pair of dungarees. But nor is there anything inherently oppressive in any of these items of clothing – what matters is the freedom of personal choice. In the UK, the majority of Muslim women, like myself, have made a personal decision to wear the hijab, whereas others have chosen to wear the niqab; it is not something that has been forced upon us by our husbands, our fathers or anyone else.

From the early seventh century to the present day, women have been instrumental in shaping Islamic history; a fact that has not been widely recorded in historical narratives. It has been suggested that this is because these narratives were written by Muslim male exegetes, which have marginalised or silenced women's contributions. Khadija, first wife of the Prophet Muhammad, believed in the message of the Quranic revelations in 610 CE, even before Muhammad understood himself to be a prophet of God. Khadija's wealth, inherited from her merchant parents, allowed him the freedom to meditate, and she offered reassurance regarding the authenticity of his first revelations. Then there are the countless examples of Muslim women who have made outstanding contributions to science, medicine and politics. Zubayda bint Ja'far al-Mansur pioneered the monumental project of digging wells and building reservoirs all along the pilgrimage route from Baghdad to Mecca in the late eighth and early ninth centuries; Fatima al-Fihriya was a patron of art and buildings who in 859 CE founded Al-Qarawiyin mosque, which later became one of the oldest universities in the world; Sutayta al-Mahamili was a tenth-century mathematician and an expert in jurisprudence; Maryam al-Ijliya al-Astrulabiya made astrolabes used for land navigation and time telling in the late 900s; and Dhayfa Khatun excelled in management and statesmanship in the thirteenth century. Our history is richly strewn with women of all cultures and religions who would be called feminists in today's terms, yet despite this, women across the world still face discrimination battles because of their gender. In *The Book of the City of Ladies*, fifteenth-century writer Christine de Pizan challenged the misogynistic attitudes towards women and their role in the Middle Ages. Years later, during the Enlightenment, writers and philosophers such as Margaret Cavendish, the Duchess of Newcastle-upon-Tyne, and Mary Wollstonecraft, author of *A Vindication of the Rights of Woman*, argued passionately for greater equality for women.

Today, younger Muslim women are serious about their educational and professional goals and are performing exceptionally well educationally. They are determined to break out of the traditional mould to enter the workforce and promote a more cohesive society.

Britain should be inspired by the women leading the fight against gender inequality, harassment and discrimination; women who get up more times than they are knocked down. Women who refuse to give up. Women who are determined to fulfil their potential. Though some of us may choose to wear the veil and some do not, we all face the same battle against prejudice and stereotyping that seeks to limit our potential simply because we are women. Our experiences differ, but our hopes do not.

And in place of simple identity politics, we need an awareness of how multifaceted we all are. No one is solely 'Muslim' or 'white'; we occupy so many spaces – gender, age, race, faith, but also upbringing, worldview, interests, hopes and dreams. As our society grows more multicultural, we borrow from each other, we find different ways of expressing our own beliefs and cultures, and rather than becoming one great monocultural blob, diversity multiplies exponentially. My Islam is British and Bangladeshi at the same time. I am irrevocably a product of multiculturalism, which is why the Islamophobia I see every day is a threat to both my British identity and my Islamic faith, and to every part of my being. That's part of why I feel the need to defend the veil.

I have campaigned with women from many backgrounds on various issues, including childcare and the gender pay gap. As is the case with many women, Muslim women have to juggle demanding household tasks, childcare and work. When I had my eldest daughter in 1995, I worked for Bethnal Green Challenge as the women's initiatives co-ordinator and led on the first women-only lifeguard training, a tailored women's youth and development programme and business support for women. Childcare provision was expensive and dire, so I eventually opted to become self-employed to enable me to juggle both jobs, managing work and ensuring that family members could help to look after my daughter. My manager was very understanding and together we found a way for me to continue to work on projects I had instigated.

Even though government has developed initiatives to help women back into work after having children, and work is more accessible to women today than in previous decades, they still face childcare challenges. Childcare costs are overwhelming and are continuing to rise, and those lucky enough to find a registered childminder still have to be prepared for days when the childminder might be ill or on holiday. While salaries have remained stagnant, childcare costs have continued to rise.

From 2017 to 2018, I worked on a campaign with many other women in Tower Hamlets to stop the Labour mayor's proposed closure of the treasured council-run nurseries. We were a collection of women drawn from different political groups, colours and ages who blended together in one united team, with a few men supporting us. As the campaign grew, local politicians didn't want to be in the same room as me when I asked pertinent (they would say impertinent) questions about the closure.

As council group leader, I also brought a gender pay gap motion to full council so that women of all backgrounds could have an opportunity to be paid as equals to their male counterparts. For women across Britain to strive for adequate childcare and pay parity is a commonality across our brilliant colours.

I am proud to serve the East End that has provided a welcome to immigrant communities for generations, whether it has been Huguenots fleeing religious persecution in the sixteenth and seventeenth centuries, the Irish fleeing famine in the nineteenth century or Jews fleeing the Nazis in the twentieth century. The voices of compassion are challenging the refugee narrative; the East End is an example of settlement, assimilation and respect.

At the time of writing, I've been the councillor for Shadwell for ten years. In my first year, I campaigned for the Cable Street Mural to be restored to its original glory. The mural, originally started by Dave Binnington, was begun in 1979 to commemorate the Battle of Cable Street on 4 October 1936. Sometime after Binnington began painting it, it was daubed with racist slogans, so he abandoned the work. It was then redesigned and repainted by Paul Butler, Ray Walker and Desmond Rochfort before being unveiled in 1983 as a powerful symbol of the East End's continuing fight against fascism.

During the Great Depression of the 1930s, unemployment and homelessness soared. The manufacturing and tailoring industries, two major areas of employment for Jewish people in the East End, were particularly badly affected. Although many lived in desperate poverty, with overcrowding rife, outdated stereotypes of Jews as money-lenders and rogue landlords prevailed, and some neighbouring communities began blaming the Jewish community for deprivation in the East End. The British Union of Fascists (BUF), led by

Sir Oswald Mosley, exploited these tensions by pitching one community against another, fuelling antisemitism.

As a known Nazi sympathiser, it was widely assumed at the time that, had the Nazis successfully invaded the UK, Mosley would have been installed as head of a pro-German puppet regime. British fascists of the day described Jews as 'rats and vermin from the gutter of Whitechapel'.

The Battle of Cable Street, as it became known, began when Mosley and the BUF staged a provocative march through Stepney, home to some 60,000 Jews. The government refused to ban the march, but east London's Jewish community and their allies, including Irish dockers, local Labour and Communist parties and antifascist groups, blocked the streets, chanting, 'They shall not pass!', and succeeded in disbanding the march.

The battle prompted the passing of the Public Order Act 1936, which required political marches to obtain police consent.

Despite the antifascists' success in confronting the BUF on that day in 1936, and despite the gains made since then, it's easy to overestimate how much progress we have made. Although such blatant and public shows of racism may not be tolerated today, that does not mean it has been eradicated. On the contrary; stereotypes take a long time to break down, and people still harbour views that they could not express publicly without being convicted. Although we need to take a stronger stance towards those who disseminate false information via social media platforms and promote hatred towards minority groups, it is not enough just to tell people what they can and can't say, because that does not change how they feel; we must also educate people and actively break down these social barriers, to erase inaccurate views and reject the pigeon-holing of certain races, religions and ethnicities. At the same time, it's essential that we implement a zero-tolerance policy towards any form of hate speech, or demonisation of certain faiths or religions. We do not have to agree with someone's beliefs, but that does not mean that we cannot live alongside each other in harmony while respecting our differences.

In 2021, as we begin a new era out of the EU, face uncertainty with Covid-19 and work to address racial disparity through the Black Lives Matter campaign, there are still many lessons to be learned from the Battle of Cable Street. We must fight back against the demonisation of immigrants and people from ethnic minorities, continuing the work of those who fought to defend their community against the fascist influence. We must also recognise that immigrants and people of colour make valuable contributions not only to the British economy but to British society as a whole, playing a vital role in the NHS and other essential services. We have seen many frontline workers from minority ethnic backgrounds disproportionately affected by Covid-19. We have seen shocking police brutality, both in the US, as highlighted by the murder of George Floyd, and here in the UK.

The Cable Street Mural serves as a reminder of the lessons we have learned, not least the importance of standing together as equals to drive out intolerance and hate from right-wing extremists. The protesters' chant of 'They shall not pass' in 1936 holds true today.

Yes, we still face challenges today and will do so in the future, but that is life. It will never be easy being a Muslim woman, particularly in the Western world. George W. Bush and Tony Blair's war on terror unwittingly promoted and licensed anti-Muslim hate crimes. Unfortunately, this legacy still exists. On the day we commemorated the 9/11 attacks in 2020, my eleven-year-old nephew faced a white boy who called him a 'curry muncher', followed by, 'I'll rub your rug with my feet and then you can pray on it.' Understand-ably, my nephew impulsively reacted with anger and a fight ensued, but he was less frightened of facing up to the bully and more worried that his white teacher would not believe him and he would get a detention.

Schoolchildren's views are very much guided by their parents, and they will absorb prejudice when they see it at home, adopting it as their own. In a *Telegraph* article in 2018, it was reported that many Muslim parents were choosing to home-school their children because of the racist bullying they faced at school. In the same year, *The Guardian* report-ed that a record number of children in the UK had been excluded from school for racist bullying.

Just before the lockdown, my primary-aged niece listened as a classmate told other girls in a playground group not to talk to her because she was a Muslim. Her friend stood up for her, telling the girl to leave my niece alone. My niece walked away from the group and her friend followed her a couple of minutes later.

My niece's friend comforted her and said, 'Don't worry. I told them that you aren't a Muslim.'

My niece looked up at her friend, smiled and said, 'But I *am* a Muslim. I'm a Muslim girl.'

My niece is proud of her identity and didn't feel that she should have to lie in order be accepted. Although her friend said what she did out of kindness and concern for my niece, it is another example of Muslim girls and women feeling pressured to conceal their religion to avoid judgement. This pretence and secrecy will not change anything. Only by proudly standing up for who and what we are can we ever hope to eradicate misunderstanding and discrimination, to live in a world where we are all seen as belonging to the same human race, regardless of individual identity.

Perhaps ironically, it was Tony Blair (now executive chairman of the Tony Blair Institute for Global Change) who recently wrote: 'Many of those suffering from discrimination, like young Muslim women, still prove hopeful and resilient. These are the feelings we must foster, to build this same resilience in those who are less sanguine. Positivity, diversity and critical thinking are a bulwark against dangerous ideas.'

My children, future grandchildren and I will inevitably continue to listen to debates about the material we choose to wear on our heads, or the material our friends choose to wear on their faces. We will continue to be asked why Eid is like Christmas Day but falls on a different date each year and why Muslim women choose not to shake hands with men, along with many other questions. But the point is that we can still live alongside each other in harmony while respecting our differences, because regardless of faith, gender, race or disability, we are all different; no two people will ever be exactly the same, not even identical twins.

Perhaps one day we won't face these questions any more, but in the short term all we can hope for is that the challenges we face are limited to verbal questioning, rather than unjustified physical assaults, which sadly still occur. Back in 2009, a Muslim woman in Leicester had her niqab torn from her face by a 29-year-old man. Rehana Sidat, who runs a drop-in centre for people with learning disabilities, was born in the UK and has lived in Leicester for most of her life. Although the assailant was ordered to pay Rehana £1,000 in compensation and received a sixteen-week jail sentence, it was insignificant compared to the long-term emotional effects on Rehana, as she felt 'invaded and scared to walk down the street alone'. During the investigation and court hearing, she said she had felt like giving up but had kept going to encourage other victims to come forward.

In 2019, in the wake of the attack on a mosque in Christchurch, New Zealand, I participated in a BBC *Woman's Hour* programme which mentioned the difficulties that Muslim women who wear the hijab face in an era of heightened tensions. I mentioned a discussion I had with my eldest daughter, Zakia, in which she asked me whether I was going to be OK wearing the scarf in public. I told her that we were fine and that we have to be strong. When we look around at people extending the hand of friendship to Muslim women around the world, such as Jacinda Ardern, Prime Minister of New Zealand, we see that although there is vulnerability, there is also hope.

I mentioned earlier that following the Christchurch attack, someone left a bouquet of flowers outside Chatham Mosque with the message: 'We stand with you. We are saddened by your loss.' That act of kindness sends a huge message to people, particularly Muslim women who feel very vulnerable, and especially older Muslim women, whose first language is often not English. That message told my mother, for one, that she was not alone, that there are people here standing with her.

1 February 2013 marked the first annual World Hijab Day, a movement created by New York resident Nazma Khan, who moved to the US from Bangladesh at the age of eleven. The aim of the day was to foster tolerance and understanding by inviting non-Muslim women and non-hijabi Muslims to experience wearing the hijab for one day. The movement's website features stories of empowerment from women, including a non-Muslim woman who chooses to wear the hijab. One woman said, 'My hijab is the most empowering garment I ever had.' Another said that the Muslim ban (Donald Trump's executive order banning people from six Muslim-majority countries from entering the US) led her to Islam in 2017, saying that it gives her strength and makes her feel free.

My hope is that, together, we will drive out propaganda, empower women to be themselves, unashamedly, and show the world that women who wear the hijab are tremendously courageous, strong and proud.

As I look to the future, with my children and my siblings' children growing up and moving on, it is crucial for our generation to challenge stereotypes surrounding race, culture and religion. We must move the focus away from people's obsession with Muslim women's clothing and what it means, and instead recognise the immense fortitude they have shown in rising above Islamophobia and discrimination to lead fulfilling and successful lives.

As Sandy Dahl, wife of Flight 93 pilot Jason Dahl, wrote: 'If we learn nothing else from this tragedy, we learn that life is short and there is no time for hate.'